PAGEMILL

in easy steps

Nick Vandome

COMPUTER
STEP

In easy steps is an imprint of Computer Step
Southfield Road. Southam
Warwickshire CV47 OFB. England

Tel: 01926 817999 Fax: 01926 817005
http://www.computerstep.com

Notice of Liability
Every effort has been made to ensure that this book contains accurate
and current information. However, Computer Step and the author shall
not be liable for any loss or damage suffered by readers as a result of
any information contained herein.

Trademarks
PageMill® is a registered trademarks of Adobe Systems Incorporated.
All other trademarks are acknowledged as belonging to their
respective companies.

Printed and bound in the United Kingdom

ISBN 1-84078-086-X

Contents

Introducing PageMill

PageMill is an easy-to-use Web authoring tool that offers powerful and effective editing options. This chapter explains the basics of the program and gives some tips for creating eye-catching Web pages.

Covers

Chapter One

WYSIWYG explained

Further details about PageMill, including a tryout version for downloading, can be found on the Adobe Web site at www.adobe.com/

Adobe PageMill is the type of Web authoring program that is grouped under the acronym WYSIWYG, an acronym much loved by the computer industry. It stands for What You See Is What You Get, which means that what you layout on the screen is what the user will see when they view your site on the World Wide Web. This has been a huge leap forward for Web authoring tools and it means that the creation of Web pages is as easy as producing hard copy publications such as magazines or newspapers.

In PageMill, the elements of a Web page appear in a browser just as they are created on screen

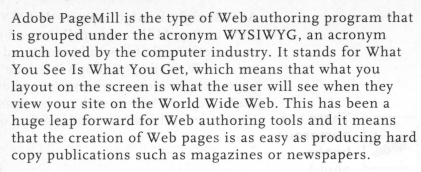

When you are viewing your pages on an Internet browser, make sure that you do so on both Microsoft Explorer and Netscape Navigator. This is because different browsers sometimes display various features in different ways and this may not be exactly the same as the way it is shown in PageMill.

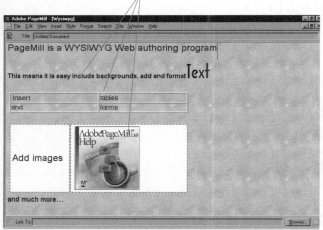

The most obvious advantage of a WYSIWYG program is that if you are familiar with a word processing or desktop publishing program then it will be second nature to insert text and images to create your Web pages. This means that you do not have to have any knowledge of HyperText Markup Language (HTML). This is the code used to create pages for the Web and it could be described as the language of the Web. But WYSIWYG programs like PageMill create all of the HTML in the background and users can be blissfully ignorant of its existence, if they so desire. However, there are certain advantages in knowing at least the basics of HTML.

Goodbye to HTML?

There are numerous books about HTML and an excellent introduction to the subject is 'HTML in easy steps'.

At first sight it might appear that WYSIWYG programs such as PageMill could spell the end of the road for HTML as something that has to be mastered by anyone wishing to create a Web site. Although it is true that excellent Web pages can be created without any knowledge of HTML, there are good reasons why it is advantageous to have at least a general idea of what is going on behind the scenes:

• Sometimes it is easier to add subtle editing touches in the source HTML code rather than in the WYSIWYG editor

• If you know the basics of HTML then you will understand why the program can do certain things but not others

• Knowing the mechanics of the program will increase your knowledge and confidence in the overall Web authoring process

PageMill has a Source mode which allows you to create and edit the source HTML code. Although this may seem a little daunting at first it is not as intimidating as it looks. HTML is not a full-blown computer language but rather a code that instructs a browser how a particular Web page should be displayed. These instructions range from the basic, such as inserting a new paragraph, to the more complicated code for creating an interactive form.

HTML code is placed between tags that give instructions relating to that particular item. For example, to create bold text the following piece of HTML would be used: <b> This gives bold text</b>. In general, each separate piece of code has an opening and a closing tag.

The basics of HTML can be picked up in a couple of hours and this will add an extra dimension to your Web authoring skills. You may want to learn a bit of HTML before you begin with PageMill or you may prefer to use the program for a while to see if the urge to learn some of the mechanics takes hold. Either way it is a good idea to learn some HTML, if only to keep up with computer buffs who like to practice a bit of one-upmanship.

The Web is an excellent resource for learning about HTML — type 'HTML' into a search engine and then sit back and work through the thousands of sites.

The basics of good Web design

The Home Page is the one that the users will see every time they log on to your site. It is therefore important that you revise and update it regularly, so that they do not get bored. However, try and maintain a recognisable theme or style.

Make sure that there are plenty of links back to the Home Page. This way people will not feel they are lost in the middle of your site.

Do not use more than three fonts on a single site and try to use proportional fonts, such as Arial.

Keep it simple

Even if you are using the most sophisticated Web authoring tool on the market, this in itself is no guarantee that you will produce top quality Web sites. It is easy to get carried away with the power and features of a program such as PageMill and try to incorporate everything at once. If you feel like this, try to resist the temptation to scatter the latest Web wizardry throughout your pages. As your Web authoring career develops, you will have ample opportunities to indulge your creative side. But initially, keep it simple.

The Apple Web site is an example of a simple, yet sophisticated and effective design. Each element on the Home Page links to another part of the site and it is elegant, clear and uncluttered

The ultimate aim of Web authoring is to get your pages noticed. In addition to keeping the overall style of the site clear and straightforward, do not be afraid to add a few more dynamic elements for effect. These could include animations, scrolling text, or images that change from one to another. The golden rule is to not get carried away with these elements, and to use them sparingly.

Always check your links from one page to another. If these are broken then the user may become disillusioned very quickly indeed.

Try and avoid too many bright colours. These may look effective at first but they can becoming irritating.

White is excellent for Web page backgrounds. Use this as a specific design option and actively select white for the background colour.

Developing a site

When you are putting together a Web site a reasonable degree of planning will pay considerable dividends in the long run. Begin by considering the following points:

- Who is the site for? If you are designing a corporate intranet you will have to have a very different design from someone who is working on a site for the latest teenage boy band

- Is the site for information or entertainment?

- Will you have an interactive element on your site in the way of on-line purchases or surveys?

- Is there a timetable for revising and updating?

- Do you have a design theme that will be recognisable throughout your site?

The Web site of Adobe, the makers of PageMill, is a good example of combining a lot of information on a site that is still pleasing to look at:

The logo ensures consistency throughout the site

A Navigation Bar appears on every page

One main image draws attention to that item

White space is used so that the page is not overcrowded

A mixture of textual and graphical links is used

Installing PageMill

PageMill is usually provided on a CD-ROM and the minimum requirements to run it are:

Macintosh

- PowerPC processor
- System 7.5.5 or greater
- 8 Mb of available RAM
- 23 Mb of available hard disk space
- 8-bit, 256 colour display or greater
- CD-ROM drive

Windows

- Any 80486 or greater processor
- Microsoft Windows 95 or Windows NT 4.0 or later
- 16 Mb of RAM for Windows 95 or Windows NT
- 20 Mb of available hard disk space
- VGA (8-bit or higher) or higher-resolution monitor, 800 x 600 recommended
- CD-ROM drive

Custom setup

One option when installing PageMill is to choose certain parts of the program.

 PageMill can also be obtained by downloading it from the Adobe Web site at www.adobe.com/

 When you instal PageMill for the first time it is best to select the full installation. When you are more familiar with the program you may want to instal the custom version.

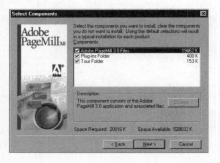

The custom installation option can be useful if there are parts of the program you do not require

Macintosh and PC versions

PageMill predominates on the Macintosh (Mac) but it is equally at home on this and the PC format. However, due to its position in the Mac market the majority of the screenshot examples in this book will be for PageMill in Mac format. But Adobe have designed the program so that the majority of the views contain almost identical commands and menus.

One area of difference between the Mac and the PC versions of PageMill is where there are menus with several panels within them. The Mac version shows this with icons in a scroll bar down the side, while the PC version has tabs along the top of each menu. One instance of this is the Preference menus, which are looked at in Chapter Two.

PageMill menus, such as this one for inserting items onto a page, are virtually identical between the Mac and the PC platforms:

Mac   PC

The commands (such as Select>File) throughout the book will be for both formats unless specified otherwise. If there is a difference, then the Mac version will come first, with the PC version in brackets beside it. If the screen shots for a particular function vary significantly, or there is one important difference, then both versions will be included.

On both the Mac and the PC platforms there are a number of ways to perform each task. For the sake of simplicity, I have included one for each task, usually selecting the options from the toolbar. A list of the most common shortcuts is included on the Handy Reference page on the inside front cover of the book.

Mac and PC users will notice very little difference between the two formats for PageMill, although it is worth remembering that Macintosh made its reputation largely with design and publishing tools.

Edit mode

Preview mode

There are three main modes in PageMill and the one in which most of the page creation is done is Edit mode. This is the default mode that appears when PageMill is opened and it is the mode in which the content is usually added.

 The Switch mode button allows you to toggle between Edit mode and Preview mode.

The Menus

The Toolbar

The Switch to Preview mode button

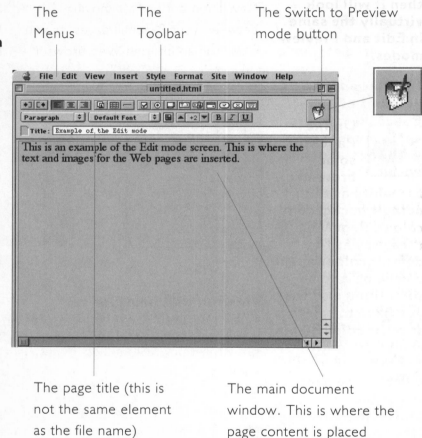

 Content can also be added in Source mode but this requires some knowledge of HTML. Familiarise yourself with how Edit mode works before you try this.

The page title (this is not the same element as the file name)

The main document window. This is where the page content is placed

Preview mode

If your page has basic text and images then it will look virtually the same in Edit and Preview modes.

Unlike PageMill, some browsers use white as their default background colour. PageMill uses grey as the default colour and if you want it to be something else then you have to select a specific colour. This can be done with the Inspector palette (see page 19) or the preference settings (see page 24).

Preview mode enables you to see how your page will look when viewed on the Web. This is particularly useful if you have animated elements or items that are running a script such as JavaScript.

Navigation buttons for moving between your PageMill pages, as you would on an Internet Web browser

Switch to Edit mode button

The main document window looks similar to Edit mode, although there could be differences, depending on the type of content added

Viewing in a browser

As a final check for your page you can view it in a Web browser, if it has already been saved. This will give a definitive view of how it will appear when it is published.

To view a page in a browser, select View (from Edit or Preview mode)

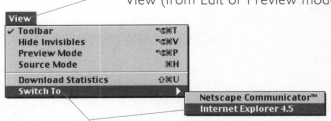

2 Select Switch To and then choose the required browser

Source mode

Source mode is a useful option if you have a reasonable grasp of HTML and you want to change something on the page that does not seem to want to co-operate in Edit mode. Sometimes it is easier to make the changes in the source HTML. To work in Source mode:

Source mode can only be accessed from Edit mode. It is the HTML behind the content on the Edit mode page.

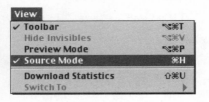

Select View>Source Mode

Source mode is useful for seeing how your pages are created. Take the time to learn a bit of HTML and then look at the source of your pages. This will help if you want to edit your HTML in future.

Source mode appears. It has similar menus and toolbars to Edit mode, since it performs a similar task, only this is a behind-the-scenes view

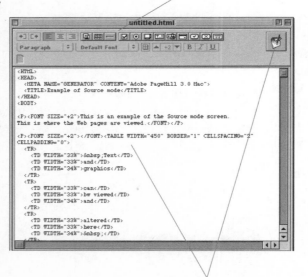

Switch back to Preview mode to see how the page has altered.

The HTML code can be edited within Source mode. Any changes that are made here affect the layout of the page

The toolbar

The toolbar is available in Edit mode or, partially, in Source mode and can be used to insert and format elements on your Web pages.

 The toolbar can be hidden by selecting View and then clicking Toolbar so that the tick next to it disappears. This can be useful if you want to increase the area of your document window.

The toolbar should be visible by default in Edit mode but if not, do the following:

Select View

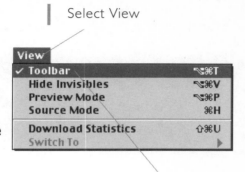

2 Select Toolbar. (If there is a tick next to it, it is already active)

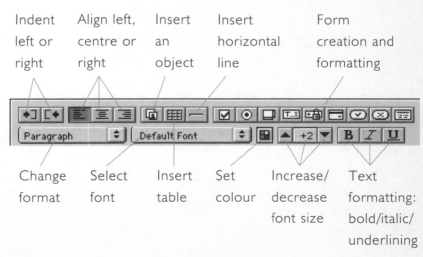

In Source mode the toolbar is visible but most of the functions are greyed-out which means they cannot be selected. The only functions which are available are the ones for inserting objects, tables and horizontal lines and also the form formatting functions.

The toolbar appears at the top of the screen:

Indent left or right

Align left, centre or right

Insert an object

Insert horizontal line

Form creation and formatting

Change format

Select font

Insert table

Set colour

Increase/ decrease font size

Text formatting: bold/italic/ underlining

The menus

The PageMill menus contain all of the functions that are needed to open, create, format and save Web pages. They operate in the same way as the menus in the majority of popular software programs: click on the main heading of the menu and then a drop-down list will appear with the various options for that heading. In some cases the options may be greyed-out, indicating that they are not available.

The PageMill menus and their general uses are:

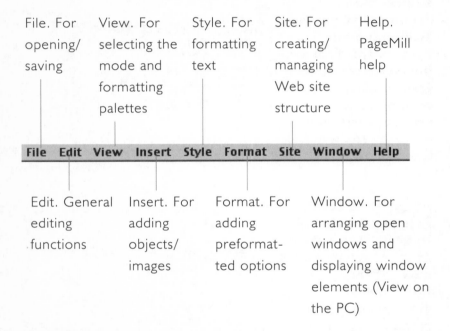

File. For opening/ saving

View. For selecting the mode and formatting palettes

Style. For formatting text

Site. For creating/ managing Web site structure

Help. PageMill help

| File | Edit | View | Insert | Style | Format | Site | Window | Help |

Edit. General editing functions

Insert. For adding objects/ images

Format. For adding preformat-ted options

Window. For arranging open windows and displaying window elements (View on the PC)

Shortcuts

The Windows version of PageMill also has the Search options as a separate menu.

A large number of menu options have shortcuts so that the functions can be accessed through a combination of key strokes. The most common ones are included on the Handy Reference page on the inside front cover. Due to constraints on space the menu options referred to throughout the book will be for selecting them from the menu option lists rather than the shortcut keys. The various options will be discussed more fully in each relevant section.

The Inspector

The Inspector is a floating palette that allows changes to be made to a variety of page attributes and preferences. In Edit mode this can be accessed at any time during the Web page creation process. To show the Inspector:

The Inspector palette can be moved around the document window by clicking on the border at the top of the palette and then dragging and dropping it to a new location. This is useful if you want to work on a particular part of the screen that would otherwise be obscured by the Inspector.

Select Window>Show Inspector (View>Show Inspector in Windows)

There are four sections on the Inspector palette and these will be dealt with in greater detail in the relevant chapters. However, the most straightforward option is the Page one.

Frame panel   Page panel   Form panel   Object panel

Page attributes can be set with the options on the right.

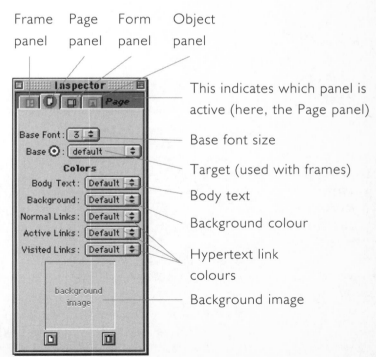

This indicates which panel is active (here, the Page panel)

Base font size

Target (used with frames)

Body text

Background colour

Hypertext link colours

Background image

The Pasteboard

The Pasteboard is an area where regularly used images or items of text can be stored and then inserted into pages when needed. This can be used for elements that are used on several pages. To use the Pasteboard:

 There are five pages for placing text and images on the Pasteboard. More than one item can be placed on each page. In the Mac version each page is accessed by clicking on the double triangle in the bottom left of the Pasteboard. In Windows the pages have numbered tabs along the bottom of the Pasteboard, which can be selected to move between pages.

1 Select Window>Show Pasteboard (View>Show Pasteboard in Windows)

2 The Pasteboard appears on the screen. Click here to move between pages

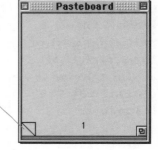

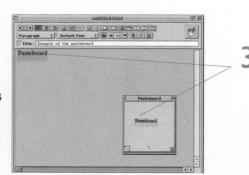

 Dragging and dropping is the only way to move items from the Pasteboard to an active page.

3 Place items by selecting them and then dragging them onto the Pasteboard

The Pasteboard will remain on screen and the items on it can be included on other pages by dragging and dropping them from the Pasteboard.

Invisibles

PageMill provides a number of elements that can be inserted during the editing process and which do not appear on the published site. These are known as Invisibles and they can be accessed by:

Select Insert – the Invisibles are listed at the bottom half of the menu

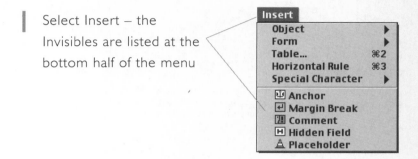

Invisibles can be shown or hidden by selecting View>Show Invisibles or View> Hide Invisibles.

Each of the Invisibles serve a different purpose:

Anchors

Anchors are used to create links to specific parts of a page. This is discussed in Chapter Seven.

Margin Breaks

Margin Breaks insert a break between an element on the page and another element below it:

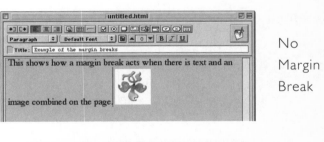

No Margin Break

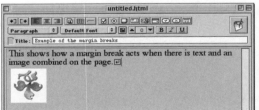

Margin Break inserted

Comments

These let you add comments relating to items on the page.

To add a comment:

 If you have any 'last updated' items on your Web site, add comments to remind yourself of a date for updating the pages.

1 Click the inserted Comment icon

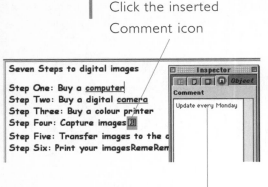

2 Add your comment (this will appear whenever the Comment icon is selected)

Hidden fields

These are used when dealing with forms. (This is discussed in more detail in Chapter 10.)

Placeholders

 Placeholders can be used for any scripting language that is not supported by PageMill but which can still be recognised by a browser.

Placeholders are used to indicate to PageMill that an item should be ignored. (This is used for items such as JavaScript and other scripting languages.) The HTML code for this is <!--NOEDIT--> and <!--/NOEDIT> and it lets PageMill know that this item is not to be changed or edited.

Once a Placeholder has been inserted, the code that it contains can be included by clicking on the Placeholder and then entering the script text in the Inspector Placeholder box.

Structuring a Web site

This chapter shows how to set up the structure for your Web site and how to create, open and close pages. It also shows how to set the preferences to determine the overall appearance of the site.

Covers

Chapter Two

Setting preferences

 Various elements on an individual page can be changed without changing the default preferences. For instance, if you want to change the background colour for one page only then this can be done through the Inspector palette.

Before you begin getting into the nitty-gritty of creating Web pages it is a good idea to select the preferences for your site. These are options that determine the settings for a variety of functions, from background colour to how active elements will be displayed on your pages. The reason that it is advisable to set your preferences at the start of the authoring process is that once they are defined, they will be the same for all pages you create and you will not have to change them when you start a new page. The preferences menus are accessed by selecting Edit>Preferences.

General preferences

These affect how your pages will be displayed.

 In Windows only, there is a general preference to set the default preview mode to PageMill Preview or to preview the page in the Explorer browser. There is also a preference for automatically saving files before they are previewed in a browser.

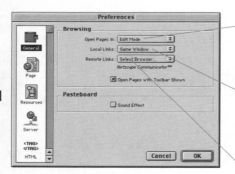

The mode in which pages will be first opened. The default is Edit mode

The location for where links will be opened. The default is Same Window

Set a browser for viewing remote links to the Web

Page preferences

These are similar to the settings on the Inspector palette:

 On pages 24-27, don't forget to click OK to confirm changes.

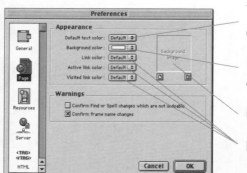

Text colour (default=black)

Page background colour (default=grey)

Background image

Link colours

Setting the HTML tag colour to a different colour to the text in Source mode is a good way to quickly identify what is a tag and what is page content.

It is best to use the default settings for font size and alignment. This is because different browsers interpret HTML in slightly different ways and these are the best settings.

Active elements are discussed in more detail in Chapter Six.

HTML preferences

These preferences affect the way the HTML code is displayed in Source mode:

Comment colour. This is for comments that do not appear when viewed in a browser; default is red

Tag colour. This is for the HTML tags; default is blue

Preferences for how the HTML specifies font size and alignment

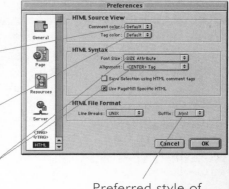

Preferred style of file extension

Active content preferences

These preferences affect the way active elements such as Java and ActiveX (Windows only) are displayed.

Enable Java Applets. This allows PageMill to run applets

Run Applets in Edit mode. This enables applets to work in Edit and Preview modes

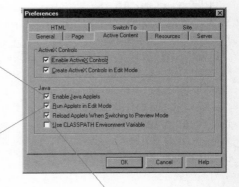

Reload. This tells PageMill to reload an applet when viewing a page in Preview mode

Resource preferences

This identifies a folder where PageMill automatically saves imported images and active elements. It can be the same folder as your Web page files or it could be a separate one.

After step 1, the Choose a Folder dialog box (Browse for Folder in Windows) appears.

| Click on the Resources folder (Browse in Windows)

2 Select a folder from your computer

Switch To preferences

The Switch To options can be viewed in any mode by selecting View>Switch To. A list of programs that are available will then appear. A file must have been saved for this to be active.

This enables you to create a custom list of programs that you can quickly access while you are working in PageMill. This could include browsers and image editing programs.

For the Mac, select the programs that you want to have as an option to switch to when you are working in PageMill

In Windows, enter the name of the programs and then use Browse to locate them on your computer

...cont'd

 If you have changed the name of the site resource folder from the default, type in the new name.

 When it comes to loading your site onto the Internet this will probably be done through an Internet Service Provider (ISP). These are companies who provide access to the Internet.

Most ISPs offer free Web space when you register with them and there are an increasing number who offer completely free access. If you are registering a site then your ISP will provide you with a Web address (URL or Uniform Resource Locator) and details about loading your site.

Site preferences

These refer to the site management function of PageMill and are discussed in more detail in Chapter Eleven.

Most of the options are for site management tasks

The site resource folder – see the HOT TIP

Server preferences

These preferences are relevant when you want to publish your site. They ensure that your local directory is a mirror of the one that is loaded onto the Web, so that there is no problem with broken or missing links.

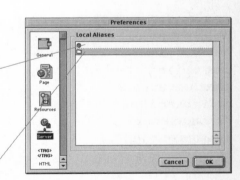

1 Enter the Uniform Resource Locator (URL or Web address) of your site

2 Enter the location of your site on your own computer. (This should ensure that all links and pathnames are correct)

Creating a new site

A Web site is a collection of pages that, when viewed in a browser, are linked together with hyperlinks. These allow the user to move from one page to another by clicking on the relevant links.

In PageMill, in addition to creating page content and links, the program can view the pages as an overall site. This then enables you to view the entire site structure so that you can see which pages are linked to each other, which objects and images are included in the site and also any errors that have occurred. This site management aspect is an essential feature, particularly for larger Web sites.

If a Web site is relatively small then you can put all of the files and images into one folder. However, for larger files it is a good idea to create separate folders for the HTML files and other items such as images, icons and Java applets.

In PageMill all pages of a Web site have to be part of a single site structure for it to be published successfully. This means that all of the items that make up the site have to be saved within a single folder, known as the site's local root folder. Theoretically, this folder could be created within the Finder management system (Explorer in Windows). However, it is important to do this within the PageMill structure so that all site elements are fully incorporated into the site structure. There are two ways to create a local root folder:

Method 1

Once a local root folder has been created this can be checked in your computer's file management system.

1 In Edit mode, select File>New>New Site (Site>New in Windows)

2 Enter a name for the root folder and a location on your hard drive where you want this folder to be located

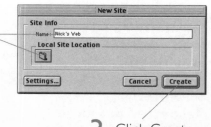

3 Click Create

...cont'd

When a new site is created, PageMill automatically creates a Home Page with the file name 'index.html'.

Once you have created a new site you can get back to the business of creating Web pages. This function really comes into its own once the site has a number of pages. A detailed view of site management is given in Chapter Eleven.

To get back to Edit mode from Site Overview, select Edit>Close (Site>Close in Windows).

Method 2

1 Select File>Open> Open Site (Site>Load in Windows) and then select an existing site

2 In the site details window, select File>New (Site>New in Windows)

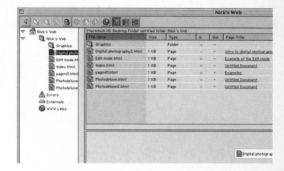

The site details window consists of the Site Overview, the List view and the Links view. These will all be discussed in greater detail in Chapter Eleven but the structure of the Site Overview is worth looking into:

Site Name. Unless this has been given a separate name it is the same as the local root folder

Local root folder. The main folder, containing all of the site elements

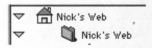

Errors folder. A folder that alerts you to any errors

Externals folder. A folder that gathers items that are outside the site structure

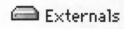

WWW links. A folder showing your site's links to external Web sites

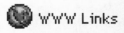

Setting preferences for a new site

Once a new site structure has been created it is possible to create a folder for any images that are imported into the site and need to be converted into a format that PageMill recognises, or any other items that are outside the site structure. To do this:

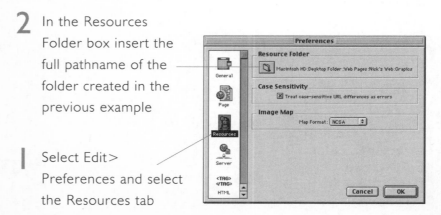

2 In the Site Resources Folder Name field, name the folder

| Select Edit> Preferences and select the Site tab

If you do not select a preference for the resources folder, PageMill does it automatically, with a folder called PageMill_ Resources.

Once this preference is set it ensures that the items will be included in the site once it is published. To make sure they are also included before the site is published:

2 In the Resources Folder box insert the full pathname of the folder created in the previous example

| Select Edit> Preferences and select the Resources tab

In the example on the right, the folder is: Web Pages: Nick's Web:Graphics.

Opening pages

Opening a new page

In Edit mode, PageMill launches with an empty document window (or file), ready to be worked on.

To create a new page:

In Windows the Open command is File>New Page.

| Select File>New> New Page (File>New Page in Windows)

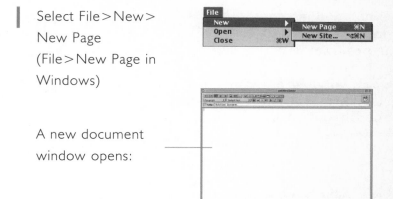

A new document window opens:

Opening an existing page

In Windows the Open New Page command is File>Open.

Once pages have been created and saved into a folder it is quick and easy to open them for further editing:

| Select File>Open> Open (File>Open in Windows)

2 Select the file that you want from the relevant directory

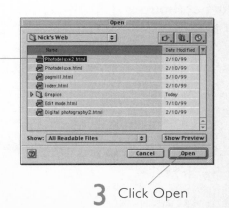

3 Click Open

Saving pages

Files in PageMill have either an .htm or an .html extension. This does not have to be included in the file name text box as the program will insert this automatically. As a rule, use .html for Macintosh and .htm for Windows.

Once you have saved a file for the first time, keep saving it throughout the editing process. This will protect your work up until the most recent save, in the event of your computer crashing.

Give Home Pages the file name of default.html or index.html as this is the format preferred by most Internet Service Providers.

When a PageMill page is first opened it will not have a specific file name: it will be called something like Untitled.html. You can either save the file immediately or add some content first and then save it.

To save a page:

1 Select File>Save Page

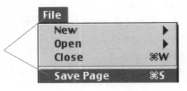

2 Select a folder for the page and give it a name

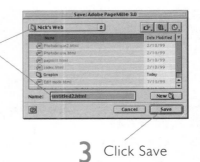

3 Click Save

Once a page has been saved, the file name appears in the title bar at the top of the screen:

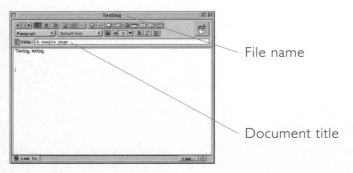

File name

Document title

This is different to the document title (the name that appears when the page is viewed on a browser). This can be the same as the file name, or it can be completely different.

Save As and Revert to Saved

 When saving a page for the first time both the Save Page and the Save As commands have the same effect. Save As can also be used once a file has already been given a specific file name.

 If you have hyperlinks to other pages on a page that has been newly created using Save As, make sure they are needed. It may be the case that they are only required on the original page.

 When using Save As, remember to change the page title as well as the file name. Otherwise the two pages will have the same title when viewed on a browser.

Save As

If you want to create two pages that have some common elements of content, or copy a page to a different location, this can be done with the Save As command:

1 Open an existing page

2 Select File>Save Page As

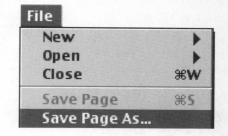

3 Select a location and a new file name for the new page

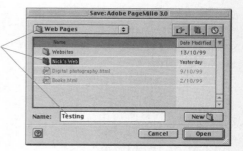

Revert to Saved

Revert to Saved can be used to discard editing changes that you have made but which you decide you do not want to keep. This is done with the File>Revert to Saved command and it removes all of the changes since the last time the page was saved.

However, if you save your work regularly (as is recommended in case your computer crashes) then you will not be able to revert to the page in the format it was when you opened it.

Closing a PageMill session

When you have finished creating and editing pages you can close your PageMill session in the same way as you would with any standard program such as a word processing or desktop publishing package. You can either close each individual page that you have been working on, or you can close the entire PageMill session.

Closing individual pages

1 Select File>Close

 If you have not already saved a file before you close it, the dialog box will ask if you want to save changes to 'untitled.html'. If you select Save (Yes in Windows) then the Save As dialog box appears and you can give the file a name and save it into the chosen folder.

2 If you have not saved the file (or have made changes since the last Save), one of the dialog boxes on the right will appear. Select Save (Yes in Windows)

Macintosh

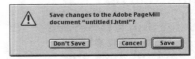

Windows

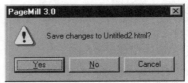

Closing a whole session

1 Select Window>Close All

2 For each file that has not been saved (or has had changes made since the last Save), the above dialog boxes appear. Select Save (Yes in Windows) for each file in turn

Working with text

Text is one of the fundamental elements of a Web page. This chapter covers adding text and basic formatting such as text size and colour. It also looks at finding and replacing text and checking spelling.

Covers

Chapter Three

Setting the background

The default page background in PageMill is grey. This is not the most inspiring colour for a Web page background and it can make it hard to read text. So before you begin adding text, choose a different colour for the page background. White is a clear, unobtrusive background and it provides an excellent contrast to dark text.

 White text can look effective on a dark background. However, it can be tiring to read if there is a lot of it.

Setting the background for all site pages

1 Select Edit > Preferences > Page

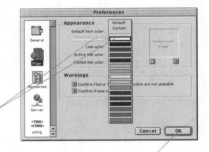

 You should try to keep a consistent background colour throughout your Web site, in order to achieve a recognisable theme. However, individual pages with a different background can be used for effect or extra impact.

2 Select Background color: and choose white

3 Click here

Setting the background for the active page only

In the Inspector, select Background: and choose white

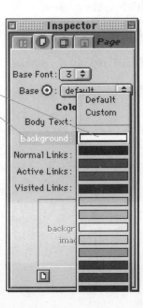

 If the Inspector is not on-screen, click Window>Show Inspector. **Click View>Show Inspector in Windows.**

Inserting text

 If you are working on a new document window and you want to start entering text halfway down it, then you will need to insert carriage returns until the cursor is in the correct position.

Text entry in PageMill is very similar to that of popular word processing programs such as WordPerfect or Word, or desktop publishing programs such as PageMaker or QuarkXpress.

To add text in Edit mode:

1 Place the cursor at the desired insertion point and start typing

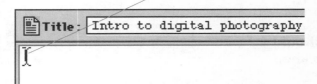

 Text can be added to existing content by positioning the cursor at the insertion point and then typing. The existing text will then move to accommodate the new content.

2 Press Return to insert a paragraph break

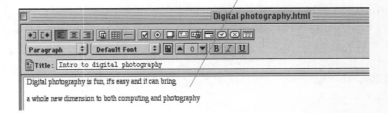

 The HTML tags for a paragraph break are <p>Text</p>. The tag for a line break is <br>. (The latter is one of the few HTML commands that does not have a corresponding closing tag.)

3 Select Insert>Special Character>Line Break to place text on the next line down. (This is a smaller break)

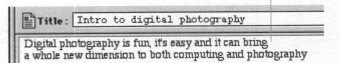

Selecting a typeface

With any visual document it is important to have variation in the style and size of the typefaces that are used. This is especially important on a Web page. Web surfers can be notoriously fickle: if a page does not make an immediate impact, they may move on without even a second glance.

The default typeface in PageMill is Times Roman but there are dozens of others available. To select a typeface:

 Do not get carried away with the array of typefaces on offer. Use a maximum of three and keep them consistent with the style of your site: a dependable font, such as Arial, for a business-orientated site and a more extroverted one for a personal site.

Type your text and highlight it

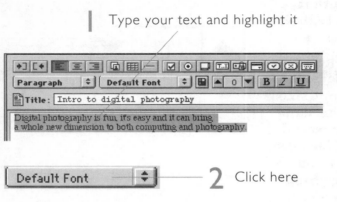

2 Click here

 People viewing your site on the Web will only be able to see the fonts that are on their own system. So if you have used a lot of unusual fonts then the effect may be lost, as they will be displayed in a default such as Arial or Times Roman.

3 Select a typeface

Sample typefaces:

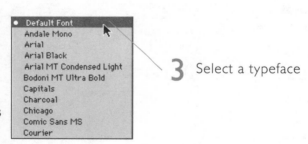

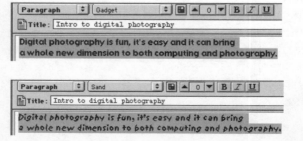

Changing text size

 The font sizes on a PageMill page are not the same as the point size. The PageMill settings are HTML commands that determine text size.

 The default font size is the same as the base font size. The Relative Font Size menu changes the font size in relation to the base font. So if the base font is 3 and +1 is selected from the Relative Font Size menu, then the font size for the selected text would be 4.

 Once the base font size has been set, the size of individual words or letters can still be changed by using the font icons above.

The size of the text on a page can be altered by selecting the text that you want to change and using the following icons on the toolbar:

Increases text by one size

Launches a menu for increasing/decreasing the relative font size

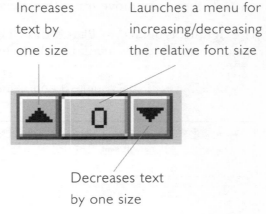

Decreases text by one size

The Inspector can also be used to set the base font size for the entire page:

Amend the Base Font here

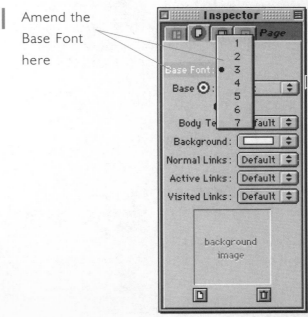

Changing text colour

To change the colour of text, do one of the following:

Method 1

Colours in HTML are denoted by a hexadecimal (hex) code. This is a combination of six letters and numbers (A–F and 0-6). Black is "000000" and white is "ffffff". To see the hex code for the colours on the Colour Panel, position the cursor over a colour and then wait a couple of seconds. The hex code will then appear in yellow.

1 Highlight the text you want to recolour

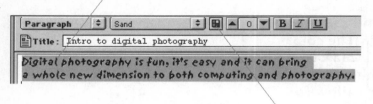

2 Select the Set Colour icon

3 Select a colour

Method 2

1 Highlight the text

In Windows, the colour panel can be accessed by selecting View> Show Color Panel.

2 Select Window> Show Color Panel

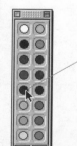

3 Select a colour

The color dialog boxes allow for more variation when choosing a colour. However, remember that some browsers view colours differently from others. If you stick to the Web standard colour palette on the facing page you can be sure that the chosen colour will be displayed correctly.
(If you create a custom colour it may not be displayed exactly the same in all browsers.)

Method 3

1 Highlight the text

2 Select Style > Color and select a colour

3 Select Custom to launch the color dialog box

4 Carry out step 5 (Mac users) – alternatively, step 6 OR 7 (Windows users)

5 Create a custom colour by adding values here and dragging the sliding scale

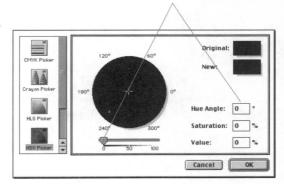

6 Select an existing colour

7 Create a custom colour by dragging these buttons

The custom colour is displayed here

Copying and pasting text

If you select Cut instead of Copy then the selection will be removed from the document window. However, it can still be pasted into a new location.

To move text from one location to another, rather than copying it, highlight the text and then drag and drop to the new location.

If you are copying and pasting text, try to do the two operations immediately after each other. Otherwise you may move on and copy something else. This will overwrite your first selection so you will have to go back and repeat the process.

Copying and pasting on the same page

Text on a PageMill page can be copied (or cut) from one location and then pasted into another part of the page. This can be done using two methods:

Method 1

1 Highlight the text and select Edit>Copy

> **Seven Steps to digital images**
> Step One

2 Position the cursor where you want the copied text to appear

> **Seven Steps to digital images**
> Step One

3 Select Edit>Paste

> **Seven Steps to digital images**
> Step One
> Step One

The pasted text appears at the insertion point

Method 2

1 Highlight the text

> **Seven Steps to digital images**
> Step One
> Step One

2 Hold down Option (Ctrl in Windows) and drag and drop the text to its new location

Copying and pasting to another page

If you have elements that are common to several pages on your site you may want to copy them from one page to another. This can be done with the first method on the facing page but there is a quicker way:

Another way to copy items onto different pages is to place them on the Pasteboard. They will then be available to paste into any active document window.

Placing items on the Pasteboard is discussed in Chapter One, page 20.

1 Open two, or more, pages and then select Window>Tile Vertically (or Horizontally)

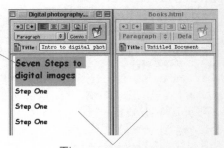

2 Highlight the text to be copied

The pages appear next to each other

3 Drag and drop from one page to another

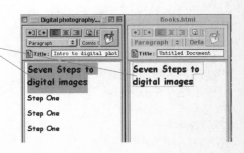

Indenting text

Aligning text

Text can be indented to leave a space on either the left-hand or right-hand side of the text. This acts like a margin.

 The HTML code for indenting text is `<Blockquote>Text </Blockquote>`. In Source mode it is possible to move the blockquote tags so that only the first line of a paragraph is indented.

However, this causes problems with the line spacing and it is not an ideal solution. If you want a paragraph with the first line indented then it is better to insert several nonbreaking spaces.

To do this, position the cursor at the start of the paragraph then select Insert>Special Character>Non-breaking Space. Repeat this until the line is sufficiently indented.

To indent text:

1. Select the text to be indented (by inserting the cursor anywhere in the relevant paragraph)

> **Seven Steps to digital images**
>
> Step One: Buy a computer
> Step Two: Buy a digital camera
> Step Three: Buy a colour printer

(In Edit mode the indent function affects the whole paragraph – i.e. a single line cannot be indented separately from the rest of the paragraph.)

2. Now perform step 3 (alternatively, step 4 OR 5) below:

3. Select Format> Indent>Indent Right (or >Indent Left)

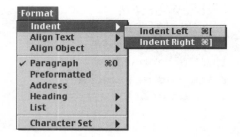

4. Click here to indent to the right

The Indent buttons in the toolbar

5. Click here to indent to the left

The text is now indented

> **Seven Steps to digital images**
>
> Step One: Buy a computer
> Step Two: Buy a digital camera
> Step Three: Buy a colour printer

Aligning text

PageMill has the three standard options for aligning text: left aligned, centred and right aligned. There are two alignment methods.

1 Highlight the relevant text

2 Perform step 3 OR 4 below

3 Click one of the alignment icons on the toolbar:

Centre align

Left align ——— Right align

HOT TIP

Whole paragraphs can be aligned by inserting the cursor anywhere within them and then selecting the necessary alignment command.

4 Select Format>Align Text, then Left, Center or Right

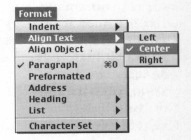

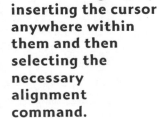
HOT TIP

Text that has been centred can be further formatted by applying the indent command to it. This increases the effect since there is a larger margin around the text.

Examples of alignment:

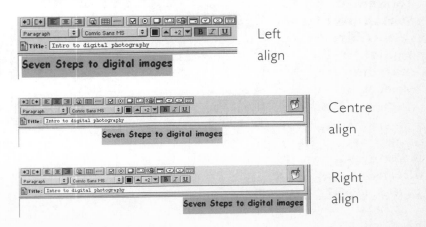

Left align

Centre align

Right align

Finding and replacing text

The Find function can also be used to look for objects and Web site addresses (URLs).

When entering criteria for a search, the constraints are:

- **Text Case — finds words with exactly the same capitalisation as the selected item**
- **Text Style — matches text with exactly the same style, such as bold or italic**
- **Whole Word — finds words as long as they are not part of another word, and;**
- **Object Size — applies to searching for objects**

When a match is found it is denoted with an outline box around it.

Finding text

PageMill can find words or phrases in a single Web page or throughout an entire site. This can be useful if, for instance, you want to locate all of the occurrences of a company name or product.

To find text:

1 Select Edit>Find (Search>Find in Windows)

2 Select Page Content

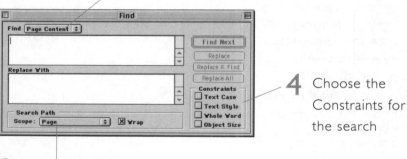

4 Choose the Constraints for the search

3 Choose the search parameters

5 Enter the item to be searched for

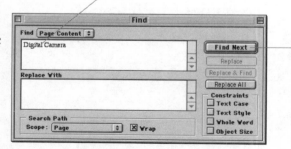

6 Select Find Next

 **If you are using Find and Replace on an entire site then go through some of the pages just to make sure that the changes have in fact been made.**

Replacing text

Replacing text in a Web site can be used for a variety of reasons:

- You may realise that you have used *there* instead of *their* throughout your site

- You may decide that you should have capitalised some words rather than have them in lower case

- If a named person, such as a Chief Executive, changes position and someone else takes over

To replace text:

1 Set up the Find function using the procedure on the facing page

 The Replace options are:

- **Replace —** replaces the next occurrence of the target text
- **Replace and Find —** replaces the target text and then looks for the next occurrence, and;
- **Replace All —** replaces all of the occurrences within the search criteria

2 In the Replace With text box, enter the text that you want to replace the original

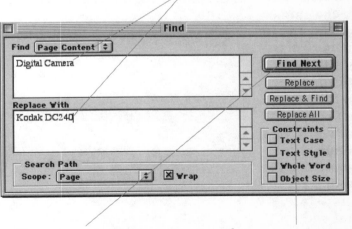

 Replacement text appears with an outline box around it:

Buy a Kodak DC240

3 Select Find Next

4 Select one of the Replace options

Checking spelling

When an unknown word is discovered the options for what to do with it are:

- **Ignore — ignores the word and then continues to check the selection**
- **Change — alters the word to the one in the Change To box or from the Suggestions list**
- **Change All — changes all occurrences of the word to the one in the Change To box or Suggestions list**
- **Ignore All — ignores all occurrences of the word, and;**
- **Add — adds the unknown word to the User Dictionary (a personalised dictionary containing words that the program dictionary does not recognise)**

The PageMill spell checker can be used to check spelling and typographical errors in a document. As with the Find and Replace function, the spell checker can be used to check a single page or an entire site.

To check spelling:

1 Select Edit > Check Spelling (Search > Check Spelling in Windows)

The Spell Checker launches:

When an unknown word is discovered the spell checker offers a Change To option and also a number of other suggested replacements

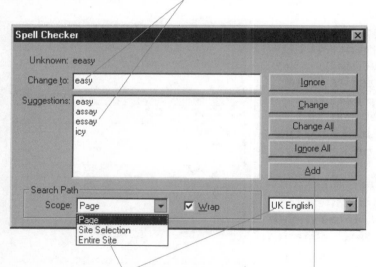

2 Use these fields to specify how much of the site to search, and the appropriate language

3 Click one of these – see the tip

Formatting text

PageMill offers a variety of formatting options to help make the textual element of a Web page visually effective. These include formatting with styles such as bold and italics, different heading sizes, formatting entire paragraphs and formatting text into lists.

Covers

Chapter Four

Physical formatting

PageMill uses two methods for formatting text: physical formatting and logical formatting. Physical formatting is the most commonly used and it changes the appearance of a particular piece of text. Once physical formatting has been applied, this will permanently set the appearance of the affected piece of text i.e. if the formatting is bold then the text will be bold in whichever type of browser the page is viewed in.

The options for physical formatting are:

Only use underlining as a last resort when you are formatting text. This is because textual hyperlinks are denoted by underlining and if ordinary text is underlined then there could be some confusion.

- Plain (no formatting)
- Bold
- Italic
- Underline
- Teletype (monospaced text)

Several types of physical formatting can be applied to a single piece of text. For instance, bold, italic, underline and teletype could all be applied to the same word or phrase.

Plain

Bold

Italic

<u>Underline</u>

`Teletype`

Examples of physically formatted text

To apply physical formatting to a piece of text:

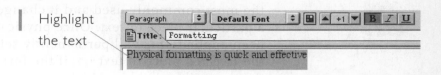

Highlight
the text

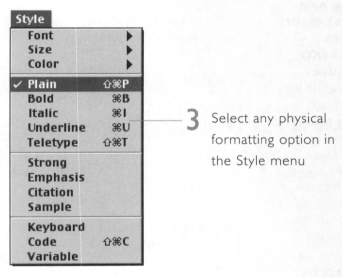

**All types
of
formatting
(physical
and logical) can be
deselected by
highlighting the
item and then
clicking on the
formatting option
so that the tick next
to it disappears.**

2 Now carry out step 3 OR 4 below:

3 Select any physical
formatting option in
the Style menu

4 Click one or more of the following icons in the on-screen
toolbar:

Bold   Underline

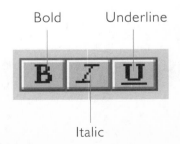

Italic

Logical formatting

For items such as bold, italic and underlining, use physical formatting rather than logical formatting. This way, you can be sure of how your text will appear when viewed on the Web. Only use logical formatting if you need it for a particular style, such as computer code.

Logical formatting allows different Web browsers to use their own definitions of how a particular piece of formatted text should appear. This can lead to confusion, as the Web author cannot be sure how a piece of logically formatted text is going to appear on a variety of browsers. The options for logical formatting are:

- Strong. Strong emphasis for text. In most cases this appears as bold but in some browsers it could be another form of strong emphasis such as underlining. However, in reality this is seldom the case

- Emphasis. Emphasis for text. This generally appears as italics

- Citation. The style for publications and reference material

- Sample. The style for computer status messages

- Keyboard. The style for text that is to be entered into a computer, such as for an online form

Physical and logical formatting can be applied to the same piece of text. For instance, you could use both Bold and Citation on a single word.

- Code. The style for displaying computer code

- Variable. Used for variables within computer instructions

Like physical formatt-ing, logical formatting can be accessed from the Style menu.

Strong

Emphasis

Citation

Sample

Keyboard

Code

Variable

Examples of logically formatted text

Applying headings

To create a heading, highlight the text or paragraph to which you want the heading size to apply and then use one of the formatting methods.

HTML has a hierarchy of six different sizes for headings. These range from H6 (the smallest) to H1 (the largest). In PageMill these are denoted by:

- Smallest heading
- Smaller heading
- Small heading
- Large heading
- Larger heading
- Largest heading

The heading commands can be accessed from the Change Format drop-down list on the toolbar:

Be consistent in the use of headings throughout your Web site. Use the largest heading size for page titles and then the smaller sizes for sub-headings.

   If you use the same hierarchy on all pages then the user will become familiar with your layout and therefore feel more confident when navigating around the site.

Click here and then choose a heading size

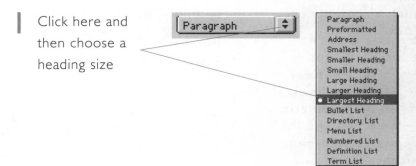

or from the Format menu:

Select Format>Heading and then the required heading size

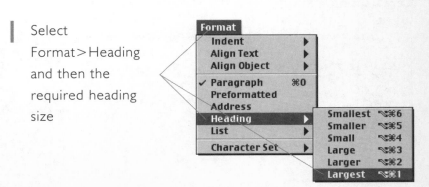

Paragraph formatting

Alternatively, use the Change Format drop-down list on the toolbar to access the same options.

PageMill has three options for formatting paragraphs: Paragraph, Address and Preformatted. These are different styles that can be applied automatically to an entire paragraph. To apply paragraph formatting:

Select Format and then one of the paragraph formatting options:

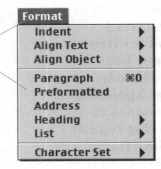

**If you use the Address formatting for an email address, you will still need to add a hyperlink to that address. Otherwise there will be no way of accessing the intended recipient.
For a detailed look at hyperlinks, see Chapter Seven.**

Paragraph option
This is the default setting and it will only need to be selected if another style of formatting has been applied to a paragraph and you want to revert to the default style.

Address option
This can be used for postal or email addresses:

1 Select the text to be formatted

As a result of steps 1-2, the text is formatted like this:

Head Office
1 High Street
Anytown
Anywhere

2 Select Address from the paragraph formatting list

When including data in a table format it is best to use the preformatted method for items that have been included from another application. If you want to create this type of item directly in PageMill then it is better to use HTML tables, which give more versatility. These are covered in Chapter Eight.

 Data for tables can easily be included from spreadsheets such as Excel. Do one of these:

- **select the data and copy and paste it into a PageMill document, or;**
- **open both programs, highlight the data and drag and drop it from the spreadsheet into PageMill**

Preformatted option

This is an excellent option for creating formatted lists, such as spreadsheet-style tables. This is done by using a fixed-width font, because the formatting can recognise multiple consecutive space characters.

Most browsers treat multiple consecutive space characters as a single space. This means that if you use the space bar to add several spaces (if you want to line up data in a table for instance) then the browser will interpret it as a single space. The preformatted format offers a more reliable way of lining up table data:

1 Import the text to (this can be done with Copy and Paste or Drag and Drop) then highlight the sections to be formatted

Sales figures - Second Quarter

	John	Sue	Steve	Brian
Apr	24	32	19	53
May	23	43	27	36
Jun	18	55	30	41

2 Select Preformatted from the toolbar Change Format drop-down list

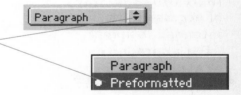

The selection now appears as a properly formatted table

Sales figures - Second Quarter

	John	Sue	Steve	Brian
Apr	24	32	19	53
May	23	43	27	36
Jun	18	55	30	41

Using lists

...cont'd

Words, phrases, sentences and even paragraphs can be made into lists. However, each item has to have a carriage return after it so that the list formatting recognises it as a separate paragraph element.

Bullet, menu and directory lists look the same when created in PageMill. It is only the uses to which they are put that are different.

As a result of steps 1-2 on the right, the text is formatted as a list:

Lists can be displayed in a variety of ways; they are a useful device for breaking up large blocks of text. Uses include:

- Price lists
- Groups of people
- Timetables
- Glossaries or indices

To access the list options select Format>List or:

> Select the Change Format drop-down list – the list options appear

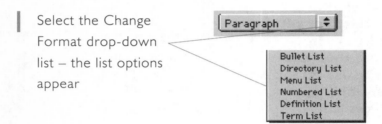

Creating bullet, menu or directory lists

These are the most common types of list; they add a bullet point to the text and then indent it to the right. To create a bullet, menu or directory list:

> Select the text to be made into a list

> 2 Select the relevant List option from the Change Format drop-down list

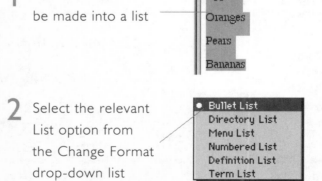

- Apples
- Oranges
- Pears
- Bananas

Nested lists

Nested lists are groups of two or more sub-lists within a main list. This can be a good way of representing sub-divisions of the information being displayed.

To create a nested list:

1 Create a list using the procedure on the facing page

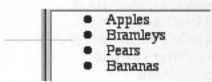

2 Highlight the item that you want to make into a sub-list of the main list

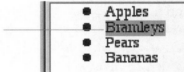

3 Select the toolbar Right Indent icon to indent the highlighted text to the next level of the nested list

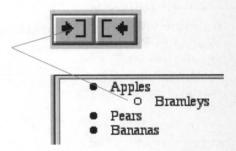

Do not get too carried away with adding levels to a nested list: if there are too many sub-lists then this may get confusing. Limit your nested lists to three levels at most for each item.

4 Repeat the process for each extra level that you want to include in your nested list

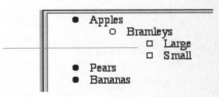

Term and definition lists

Term and definition lists are used in combination to create a style where one part is a highlighted word or phrase and the other part is its definition. This can be used for a glossary of terms or for a pen-picture description of a group of people.

To create a term and definition list:

In step 1, the term item and definition item must be in separate paragraphs.

1	Enter your text

> **Pagemill**
> An easy to use, WYSIWYG Web authoring tool. Available from Adobe it is one of the market leaders in Web authoring software.

Term and definition lists are most effective when there are several items to define. If there are only one or two then it would be just as easy to create the term item with normal formatting and then create the definition item by indenting it to the right.

2 Highlight a term element

> **Pagemill**
> An easy to use, WYSIWYG Web authoring tool. Available from Adobe it is one of the market leaders in Web authoring software.

3 Select Term List from the Change Format drop-down list

> Bullet List
> Directory List
> Menu List
> Numbered List
> Definition List
> ● Term List

4 Highlight the associated definition

> **Pagemill**
> An easy to use, WYSIWYG Web authoring tool. Available from Adobe it is one of the market leaders in Web authoring software.

5 Select Definition List from the Change Format drop-down list

> Bullet List
> Directory List
> Menu List
> Numbered List
> ● Definition List
> Term List

Term and definition items can also be created by inserting the cursor anywhere in a paragraph and then selecting the relevant list option.

A term and definition list:

> **Pagemill**
> An easy to use, WYSIWYG Web authoring tool. Available from Adobe it is one of the market leaders in Web authoring software.

Working with images

This chapter takes a general look at Web images and how to use them effectively. It also covers the specifics of inserting, formatting and editing them for Web pages.

Covers

Chapter Five

Introduction to Web images

The origins of the Internet are currently being claimed by a variety of individuals and organisations. One group that has as good a claim as any is the Advanced Research Project Agency (ARPA) in America, which created the first genuine computer network, Arpanet, in 1969.

The development of images

In the early days of the Internet and the World Wide Web it was considered a significant achievement to transfer the most basic text from one computer to another. But things have moved on significantly from the dawn of the Web, when most computers were still the size of a room. Now, with an increasingly sophisticated and media-aware audience, Web pages have to be both informative and visually appealing. Images now proliferate on the Web, whether they are photographs, icons, Clip Art, animations or complicated graphics that flash and spin before your eyes.

When the formats for Web images were being developed there were, and still are, two main considerations: quality of image and file size. The images have to be of a reasonable quality to be effective but at the same time create files that are small enough to be downloaded quickly on the user's browser.

To square this circle, the computer experts came up with two file formats that offer good quality and can be downloaded quickly: the Graphical Interchange Format (GIF) is usually used for graphics, icons and animations while the Joint Photographic Experts Group (JPEG) is best suited for photographic images.

New file formats for images on the Web are being developed, most notably the Portable Network Group (PNG). However, this is not yet as widely used as GIFs and JPEGs and there can be some compatibility issues.

When you are dealing with images for the Web there are a few points to bear in mind:

- Both GIFs and JPEGs are compressed so that the file sizes are small. Although this leads to a deterioration in quality, this is usually negligible when viewed on a browser

- GIFs can display 256 colours, while JPEGs can manage approximately 16 million colours

- A variety of other image formats can be converted into GIFs or JPEGs

The effect of images

How images are used on a Web site can greatly influence the first impressions that people have of that site. And on the Web, first impressions are vital.

Icons and graphics can be used for a more informal look

Mixing icons and photographic images can create an effective combination of the two styles. The photographic image usually captures the attention of users and the icons can be used to help them navigate around the site.

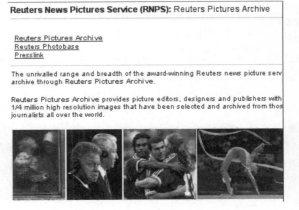

Photographic images can create a more business-like feel

Updating images

If your Web site relies heavily on graphics and images, then make sure you update them at regular intervals. A stunning image may stop Web surfers in their tracks when they first see it; but if it is still there when they access the site for the twentieth time then the initial effect will be greatly diminished. If you have a particular image that you like you can always move it to another part of the site.

Using images effectively

When you first learn to insert images into a Web page the temptation is to scatter them around like confetti. However, there are some important considerations when dealing with images:

It has been estimated that the average time Web users are prepared to wait for a page to download is 17 seconds. As the technology improves this figure will decrease steadily. It is therefore vital that your images are as lean as possible.

- The more images you include, the longer it will take to download your site. Web surfers are notoriously fickle people when it comes to downloading time

- Images can be used as the background to a Web page and can also be used independently

- Keep the physical size of the images as small as possible. Again, this affects the downloading time

- Limit the use of animations or images that spin, blink or flicker. While this can be effective in small doses, it can leave the user feeling bewildered if it is overdone

- Use each image for a specific purpose, not just because you can

- Do not use images that could be deemed offensive or derogatory

- Achieve a consistent theme by using the same image throughout your site. This could be a company logo, like the one that appears on the pages of the Apple site:

GIFs

The GIF format

The GIF (Graphics Interchange Format) file format is a versatile and popular option for a whole variety of Web images. It can be used for logos, cartoons, lines, buttons, and also photographs.

A selection
of GIF
images

The file extension for the GIF format is – .gif. **This appears after the file name i.e. beach.gif.**

GIFs use 256 colours and create relatively small file sizes by discarding any image data that is deemed to be irrelevant. This makes them best suited for flat-coloured images that do not have a great deal of colour subtleties. However, GIFs can still be used for photographic images and, while the results are not as sharp as with a JPEG, the quality is generally more than acceptable.

Types of GIFs

One useful program for producing transparent and interlaced GIFs is the GIF Construction Set from Alchemy Mindworks. Try their Web site at: www.mindworkshop .com/alchemy/ alchemy/html.

There are two types of GIFs and they both have a numerical value — GIF 87a and GIF 89a. The main thing to remember about these is that one of them, GIF 89a, can be used to create images with transparent backgrounds. These are useful if you want to display the main subject of an image against a Web background rather than the image background. There are programs that can be used to create transparent GIFs but PageMill also provides this function, as will be seen later in this chapter.

GIFs can also be modified so that when the image is downloaded in a browser it appears blurred at first and gradually becomes clearer. This is called an *interlaced GIF* and it can give the impression that the image is downloading faster than a standard GIF. In reality, though, it is not, and watching a blurred image appear on screen is just as irritating as waiting for a graphic to appear in one go. PageMill can also produce interlaced GIFs.

JPEGs and other formats

JPEGs

JPEG (Joint Photographic Experts Group) is the other main file format for Web images and it is the one that, as the name suggests, specialises in photographic images.

As with GIFs, JPEGs compress the image so that the file size is as small as possible and so is quicker to download on the Web. Although the JPEG format uses an efficient compression method, there can be a slight loss of definition if an image is opened and closed numerous times.

The main advantage of JPEG files is that they can display over 16 million colours. This makes them ideal for displaying photographic images as the colour quality of the image is retained and the file size is still suitably small.

The file extension for the JPEG format is – .jpg or – .jpeg.

Other file formats

Some of the other file formats supported by PageMill are:

- BMP (Windows) (extension – .bmp); PICT (Mac) (extension – .pct); Acrobat Portable Document Format (extension – .pdf). All image formats

- Quicktime (extension – .mov); MPEG (extension – .mpg or – .mpeg); Microsoft Video (extension – .avi); Shockwave (extension – .dcr). All movie or animation formats

- AU (extension – .au); AIFF (extension – .aiff or –.aif); MIDI (extension – .mid or – .rmi); Real Audio (extension – .ra); Windows Sound (extension – .wav). All sound formats

- Java (extension – .class); Activex (extension – .ocx) – both scripting formats for running mini-programs from either PageMill or from within a browser

Even though PageMill supports the above formats, it does not mean that all browsers will support them and some of the older ones probably will not.

Using Plug-ins

Plug-ins can also be installed to display image formats that are not supported by PageMill, such as TIFFs.

(TIFF – or Tagged Image File Format – is a bitmap format which is frequently used on the Mac and PC.)

Although PageMill supports the file formats listed on the previous pages, it needs a little extra help to display some of the more complicated ones such as sound and vision files. This is done with a program called a plug-in, which helps PageMill, and the browser the page is being displayed in, interpret the type of file that is being used. The formats that require plug-ins are: PDF files, Quicktime files, Microsoft Video, MPEG, Shockwave, AIFF, MIDI, Real Audio and Windows Sound.

Plug-ins either come on a CD-ROM or they can be downloaded from the Web. PageMill uses plug-ins that are compatible with Netscape Navigator 2.0 or later and the Netscape Web site has a page for downloading plug-ins at:

- www.netscape.com/plugins/

Installing plug-ins

Close down PageMill before you put plug-ins into the Browser Plug-ins folder. Once you have copied over the relevant files you can restart PageMill.

When you have located the relevant plug-ins they can be saved into the plug-in folder that will already have been created when PageMill was installed.

1 Locate the relevant plug-in

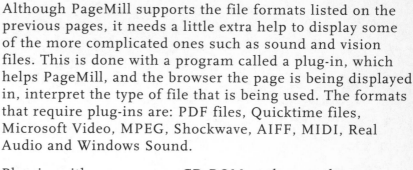

To find plug-ins on the Web, type 'plug-ins' (or the name of a specific plug-in) into a search engine and work through the results.

2 Follow the on-screen instructions to download and copy it to the Browser Plug-in folder (in either the Finder or Windows Explorer)

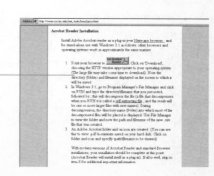

Obtaining images

From the computer

The easiest way to obtain images for your Web pages is from folders on your computer that already contain graphics or photographs. PageMill has a folder with some images already in it or you could use ones that you have on your hard drive.

 Since images are so readily available and easy to download from the Web the issue of copyright is a bit of a minefield. Some sites say that the images can be used freely, although sometimes they will ask for a link to be included to their site. Otherwise, look through the site carefully to see if there are any notes about copyright or image usage.

As a rule, for a personal site it will probably be okay to use most images, but if it is a commercial site then you will have to be a bit more careful.

Either use images from the PageMill folders, or set up your own folders for images

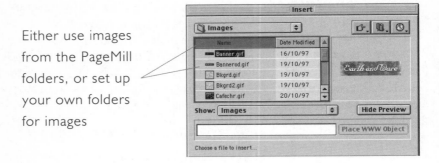

From a CD-ROM

There are several CD-ROMs on the market that have collections of thousands of images and photographs. One of the best ones to try is MasterClips, which can be previewed at the Web site: www.imsisoft.com/.

From the World Wide Web

The Web is a gold mine for images and there are numerous sites that supply a variety of GIFs, animations and photographs. In addition, if you find an image that you like you can save it to your computer by doing the following:

1 Hold down the mouse button until the menu appears (right-click on the image in Windows)

2 Select Download Image to Disk (Save Picture As in Windows)

3 Save the image to a folder on your computer

Digital cameras

In recent years the technology behind digital photography has advanced so much that it is rapidly gaining a foothold in the consumer market. Admittedly, it is still a relatively expensive hobby, but it is an excellent way to capture unique images to put on a Web site.

Shameless plug: for an in-depth look at digital photography, have a look at my own 'Digital Photography in easy steps'.

Digital cameras work by capturing a digital image on a memory card rather than a traditional roll of film. The image is then downloaded from the memory card into a computer, where it can be edited and enhanced. This way it is possible to create images of family and friends that can then be displayed around the world on the Web.

The key to digital images is the resolution i.e. the number of coloured dots (pixels) that are used to make up the image. In general, the greater the resolution then the better the image, and the more expensive the camera. However, digital images on the Web can be displayed at a relatively low resolution because computer monitors can only display a limited number of pixels per inch. This means that if you only want to capture images for online distribution you could make do with a low resolution digital camera. At current prices this would cost approximately £250–£300, but this is a rapidly evolving technology and the prices are dropping on a regular basis.

Most digital cameras save images as JPEGs by default. This means that they are ready for inclusion on a Web site.

Digital cameras are nothing to be afraid of: they look like standard compact cameras and they are easy to use

Both scanners and digital cameras usually come with software that can be used to edit the images once they have been captured.

Scanners can be fitted with adaptors to convert transparencies. These fit onto the side of the scanner; the transparency is then inserted.
   This is essential if you have a lot of transparencies that you want to include on a Web site.

Scanners

Scanners can be used to convert traditional photographs (and other items) into a digital format that is suitable for inclusion in Web pages. There are two main types: flat-bed and sheet-feed.

Flat-bed scanners look a bit like photocopiers and the document is laid on a plate of glass with a lid over it.

A flat-bed scanner

A sheet-feed scanner is like a fax machine, insofar as the document is fed into one end and comes out of the other. For most purposes, a flat-bed scanner is a quick and easy way to convert traditional photographs into digital ones. They are also reasonably cheap: £100 will buy a scanner that will suffice for the production of images for a Web page.

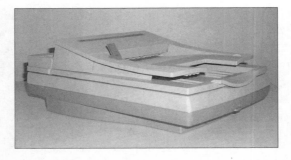

Some scanners incorporate the flat-bed and sheet-feed methods of scanning. However, these are more expensive, in the region of £300

Inserting images

Images are an integral part of any Web site and there are a number of ways to insert them in PageMill:

Inserting an image from your computer

1 Position the cursor where you want the image to be placed

2 Select Insert> Object>Image or the Insert Object icon from the toolbar

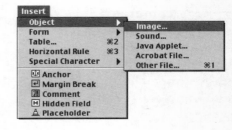

If you are inserting images from a CD-ROM then this will probably appear as the D drive on your computer. Select this and then work your way through the folders until you find the image you want.
Most image CD-ROMs offer a thumbnail view so you can preview several images at one time.

3 Click an image and select Insert (Place in Windows)

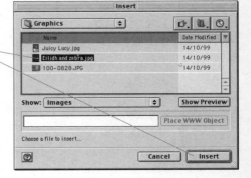

The image is placed on the page and it can then be resized or moved as desired

Inserting an image from the Web

It is possible to insert an image without even including it within your Web structure. This is done by adding it from another Web site server. This can be useful if you want to include a large image, but you do not want to store it on your own system.

To include an image from the Web:

1 Locate the image that you want to use

 Images from the Web can also be used by copying them to your own computer and then inserting them into your pages from there.

2 Identify the name and location of the image by selecting View>Source from the browser toolbar. The image location will be identified by the HTML tag: img src="image.gif":

```
<tr>
  <td width="50%" valign="top" align="cent
  <img src="gifs/ani_4_stars.gif" alt="ani.
  <td width="50%" valign="top" align="cent
```

3 In your PageMill document Select Insert>Object>Image

 In Windows, check on the Remote URL box, enter the URL and then select Link To.

4 In the Insert Object dialog box, type in the URL (Web address) of the page which the image is on. Then add the image name i.e. image.gif. Select Place WWW Object

An image placeholder appears on the PageMill page. Once the page is published and viewed on a browser, this will display the desired image

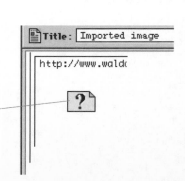

 If the source image on the Web is moved or deleted then any links to it will be broken.

Copying and pasting images

The standard Copy and Paste techniques can be used to include images on your Web pages:

The image included must be in a format supported by PageMill, preferably a GIF or a JPEG.

Images can also be copied by placing them on the Pasteboard (by either Copy and Paste or Drag and Drop) and then dragging and dropping them onto an open PageMill page.
   This method enables you to copy the same image onto numerous pages since it remains available on the Pasteboard even when you move to another page.
   See Chapter One, page 20, for details on using the Pasteboard.

1 Locate the image that you want to include. This can be in another application such as Photoshop or Paint Shop Pro or it can be on another PageMill page

2 Select the image and then select Edit>Copy

3 Insert the cursor on your active page, where you want the image to appear, and select Edit>Paste

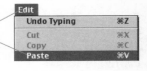

The image will appear where the cursor was inserted

Dragging and dropping

If you have created a lot of images in another application, such as an image editor, then a good way to place them on a PageMill page is to drag and drop them. To do this:

 You can drag and drop between two PageMill pages using the same technique described here.

1 Open the application where you have the images

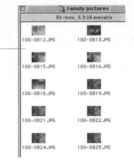

 Always keep the mouse button depressed until you are sure the image is going to be inserted at the right place. If not, it may appear elsewhere on the page.
(However, it could then still be dragged and dropped to the correct location.)

2 Open the PageMill page where the image is going to be placed

3 Resize and arrange both windows so they are side by side on the screen:

 An icon appears as you drag the image. Release this at the point where you want the image to appear.

4 Select the image and drag and drop it into the active PageMill page

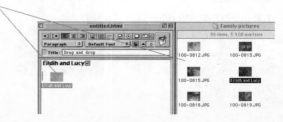

Inserting a horizontal line

Horizontal lines are an effective way to separate page content (for instance, by breaking up large blocks of text or separating text and graphics). To insert a horizontal line into a page:

Horizontal lines are a good way to separate page content and links at the bottom of the page.

1 Insert the cursor on the line above where you want the line to appear

2 Select Insert> Horizontal Rule

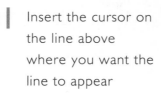

Editing the line

The Horizontal Rule option in the Object panel of the Inspector should appear automatically when the line is selected.

1 Click once on the line. (It can then be resized by clicking on one of the two resizing handles and dragging)

The Object panel in the Inspector can also be used to format the horizontal line. Implement any of the following:

Sets the width

Applies shading to the line when checked off

Sets the thickness

Resizing images

If you increase the size of an image too much then this can lead to a deterioration in the quality. It is sometimes better to use no image, rather than one that looks jagged and indistinct.

Invariably, when you insert an image into a PageMill page it is not exactly the right dimensions for the page design. However, there are two options for changing the size of an image.

Resizing by dragging

This involves physically changing the size of an image:

1. Select the image by clicking once anywhere within its borders

2. Three resizing handles appear. Click on a handle, hold down and then drag to resize the image (when you pass the cursor over a handle, it turns into an arrow)

If an image includes text, be careful not to reduce it in size too much. If you do, then the text may become difficult, or impossible, to read.

See below for details of image handles:

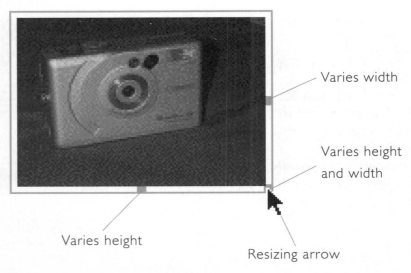

Varies width

Varies height and width

Varies height

Resizing arrow

To change the size of the image while maintaining its original proportions, hold down Shift and drag the Height and Width button.

Resizing with the Inspector

The same resizing effect created with dragging can also be achieved by using the Inspector palette. However, in this instance the image is resized by altering the numerical dimensions of the image:

 If you resize an image by dragging, the values in the Inspector change automatically.

 Pixels are the coloured dots that make up a digital image.

 The Object frame on the Inspector also has an Alternate Label box. This is for browsers that do not support a particular object or if a user has the browser setup so that it does not download images, in order to save time.
Text can be entered into this box, giving a brief description of the image.

1 Make sure the Inspector is showing. If not, select Window>Show Inspector (View>Show Inspector in Windows)

2 Select the image – the Object frame of the Inspector is activated

3 To resize to your own dimensions, check off the Scale to Height and Scale to Width boxes and enter values in the text boxes. (These can either be in pixels or as a percentage of the original size)

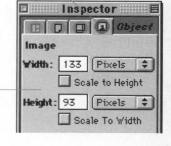

4 To resize the image proportionally, check on either the Scale to Height or Scale to Width boxes and then amend the value in the opposing text box. The value in the checked text box will then be updated proportionately

Aligning images with text

On Web pages, images and text usually reside within close proximity to each other, so it is important to be able to align your images so that they are in the right position in relation to the text. For instance, you may want to align a logo or a photograph with the heading on a page.

First, select the object you want to align. Then:

| Select Format>Align Object and select an alignment option

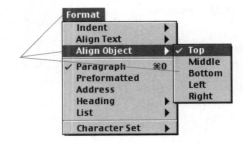

or

![elephant icon] **If there is no text, then the image can be aligned using a combination of the object and text alignment commands.**

2 Use the Align Object icons (these position the image at a specified point in relation to the text) – see below

Using the Align Object icons
Do one of the following:

| Click here to align the top of the image with the text

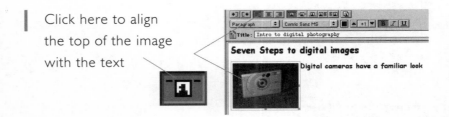

2 Click here to align the image with the text in the middle

This form of image and text alignment is best used with a limited amount of text. If you want to format several images within a large amount of text then a more effective and reliable way is to use tables. This is dealt with in greater detail in Chapter Eight .

3 Click here to align the bottom of the image with the text

4 Click here to align the image to the left of the text, which can then wrap around the image if necessary

For these alignment functions to be applied, the object always has to be selected first.

5 Click here to align the image to the right of the text, which can then wrap around the image if necessary

The Image Window

PageMill offers a variety of functions for adding elements and enhancements to images. These are Web enhancements, (for example, adding hotspots) not image editing techniques (for example, adjusting the colour).

The latter should be done in an image editing program such as Photoshop and then inserted into a PageMill document.

In PageMill, images can be worked on in the Image Window, which can be accessed by carrying out the following steps:

 There is no image cropping facility in PageMill. This has to be done in an image editing program before the image is exported to PageMill.

1   Select the image

2   Select Edit>Image>Open Image Window

The image is then shown in the Image Window:

 Hotspots are areas created on an image that then provide a hyperlink to another part of the Web site or another site. There can be several hotspots on one image.
  Hotspots are discussed in more detail in Chapter Seven.

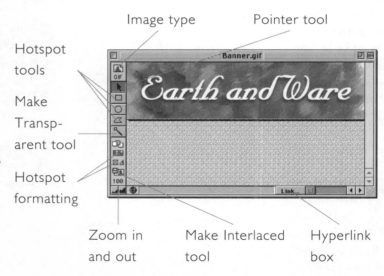

Image type   Pointer tool

Hotspot tools

Make Transp-arent tool

Hotspot formatting

Zoom in and out   Make Interlaced tool   Hyperlink box

Creating a transparent image

A useful image option in PageMill is the one to create a transparent image. This effectively removes the background of an image so that the main subject appears against the background of the Web page. There are three important points to remember about transparent images:

- They can only be created with GIF images

- They work best with a solid, one colour background since only one colour is made transparent at a time

- If part of the main subject is the same colour as the background then this may become transparent too

To create a transparent image:

JPEGs can not be converted into transparent images. However, if you open them in an image editor then you will be able to use Save As and select GIF as the file type. This will reduce the number of colours in the image to 256.

1 Select the image and open it in the Image Window

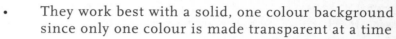

In general, flat-coloured graphics and logos are better for creating transparent images than photographs, which tend to have too much colour variation to be effective.

2 Select the Make Transparent tool, click on the part of the background that you want to make transparent then save the image

In the document window, the page background now appears behind the image

Creating an interlaced image

Some Web designers believe it is better to deliver an image a bit at a time to the user rather than have them wait until the entire image has been downloaded. This means that a blurred image appears initially and then becomes clearer as more of the image data is downloaded. This effect is created using a device called an *interlaced* GIF. Whether this is an advantage or not is up to the individual to decide, but it is a good idea to look at some pages with interlaced GIFs and see how they compare to receiving the image all in one go.

To create an interlaced GIF:

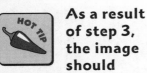

Creating an interlaced image works best with large images that take a long time to download. With smaller images the browser can usually open it before the interlacing function has had time to take effect.

1 Select an image

2 Open the image in the Image Window using Edit>Image>Open Image Window

Title: Interlaced GIF

As a result of step 3, the image should appear gradually when viewed in a browser. However, this feature is not activated when the image is viewed in Preview mode.

3 Select the Interlace tool and select File>Save Image

Dsgn4.

Make Interlaced

The same technique can also be applied to JPEG images. In this format it is called a *progressive* JPEG and it is created in the same way as an interlaced GIF.

Inserting a background image

As well as being used independently, images can also be used as backgrounds to Web pages. This adds a bit more variety than a plain colour and it can produce an eye-catching effect. However, there are some guidelines that are best followed to get the most out of this technique:

- Do not use a heavily patterned background as this could detract from the page content

- Use backgrounds that are in keeping with the overall style of the site

- Photographs can be used as backgrounds but generally only if they are in the form of a watermark. Otherwise they are too distracting

To insert an image as a background:

Always make sure that there is a good contrast between your backgrounds and your text. Otherwise the two may seem as though they are merging together and the text will become difficult to read.

If the Inspector is not displaying, click Window>Show Inspector.
(Click View>Show Inspector in Windows.)

1 In the Inspector, click here to find a background image (File in the Windows Inspector)

2 Select an image file for the background, then click Insert (Open in Windows)

The background image appears in the Inspector and in the active document

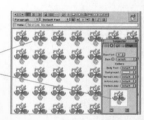

Setting preferences for backgrounds

If you select an image in the Inspector to serve as a background, this will override any background colour settings. By default, you need to specify a background image each time you open a new page. However, by using the Preferences menus, you can determine that the same image appears as a background on all pages you create.

To set the background for all pages using the Preferences menu:

It is possible to give individual pages a separate background even when the Page Preference has been set for a specific background image. Open the page that you want to alter and then select a new background image in the Inspector. Or deselect the background image — click on the dustbin on the bottom of the Inspector (Clear in Windows) — and select a plain background colour. This will not affect the background of any new or existing pages.

1 Select Edit>
Preferences>Page

2 Click here (File in Windows)

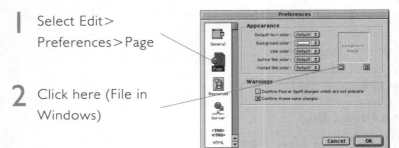

3 Select an image file

4 Select Insert (Open in Windows)

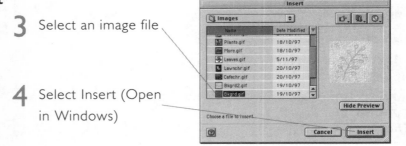

The image appears here – this will now be the background for all new pages

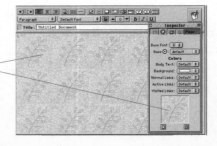

Adding multimedia

Sound and vision can give Web pages that little bit extra and make them really stand out. This chapter looks at a variety of multimedia effects, from animations to scripting languages that act like mini programs on a Web site. There are also some guidelines for using multimedia effectively.

Covers

Chapter Six

Pros and cons

Some multi-media effects, such as animation and sound, are relatively easy to create. Others, such as video and JavaScript, can be freely downloaded from the Web and it is best to stick to this approach initially.

When you first discover how to insert and create multimedia effects it is quite a thrill. But practise with them before you publish them on a Web site.

This will not only temper your initial desire to insert every element possible, but it will make you more aware of whether a certain piece of multimedia is actually relevant to your site.

In many ways, multimedia elements on a Web page are the icing on the cake. They are not essential but, if used thoughtfully, they can make the difference between a good site and an outstanding one. Conversely, if they are used to excess or without careful planning then the results could be a bewildering array of features that are an instant turn-off for the user.

Multimedia is basically anything that is not text or a plain image and it includes: animation, video, sound and scripting language that can produce a variety of special effects. This is the cutting-edge side of Web publishing and as such there are pros and cons to all aspects of it.

Visual impact

The most obvious advantage of multimedia is the visual impact it can have on the user. Static images are all very well but a moving image is guaranteed to capture the attention much more quickly. This has the advantage of getting the page or the site noticed but it can also have its drawbacks:

- A multimedia object may draw attention away from the main elements of the page. If you have a vital piece of textual data on a page you do not want someone's attention drawn away from it by a spinning graphic or a scrolling banner. If this is the case, use the multimedia object to draw the reader towards the relevant item of information rather than away from it

- If there are too many multimedia objects on a page then users will not know where to look and they may become put off by the number of items with which they are confronted

Multimedia is one area of Web design where less is definitely more. If you have one high quality item of multimedia on a page then it will stand out and draw the user into looking at what else is there. Look at some multimedia sites on the Web to see which are effective.

With most multimedia effects it is possible to include alternate text for the object that is included. This means that if a user cannot access or run the multimedia they at least have a textual explanation of what it is.

Include alternate text with multimedia wherever possible.

A simple multimedia file, such as a very small sound clip, can be well over 100 kilobytes. This compares with a GIF image that could easily be under 50 kilobytes.

Compatibility

Since most multimedia objects are effectively at the cutting-edge of Web design, some of the older browsers do not support all of them. Navigator 2.0 and Windows Internet Explorer 4.0 or later will support all but the most recent multimedia files. Earlier versions may support some multimedia effects but this is not guaranteed.

When browsers had to be paid for, compatibility with the latest Web technology was more of an issue. However, since both Netscape and Microsoft browsers are now given away free of charge, and are widely available, any Internet user can have the latest browsers for no cost and very little effort. This said, if people are using older computers then they may have trouble viewing some multimedia effects and their machines may not be able to run the latest browsers. As a rule, if it is vital that a certain piece of information is on your site then try to include it in a format other than multimedia. If it is an optional or decorative item then include it and hope that the majority of people who access the site have the more recent versions of the browsers.

File size and downloading

Working on the theory that you never get anything for nothing, it is reasonable to conclude that a file containing moving images is going to be a lot larger than one that has a static image. Multimedia files are invariably bigger in size than plain image ones and so this leads to a greater downloading time when the page is viewed in a browser. You will have to judge whether the effect is worth the risk of the user becoming tired of waiting for it to download and moving on before it has appeared. Try following these guidelines:

- Do not include too much multimedia on one page

- Always check the downloading time

- Use multimedia sparingly and for a specific purpose

Sound files

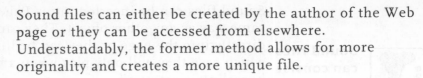

Never include vital Web page information in a sound file. This is for the simple reason that the person accessing your page may not have a sound card and speakers installed on their computer.

Sound files can either be created by the author of the Web page or they can be accessed from elsewhere. Understandably, the former method allows for more originality and creates a more unique file.

Creating your own sound files

To create a sound file you will need a microphone that attaches to your computer and a sound recording program. These range from the basic to the sophisticated and the more simple versions are usually packaged with the system software of computers that are capable of recording sound.

To create a sound file:

1 Open your sound recorder then open a new file

As the file records the sound waves are shown here

To find sites for sound files on the Web, enter 'audio files' into a search engine, or the specific type of file, such as – .au. Pay attention to any copyright or usage guidelines for the files on each site.

2 Select the Record button and then record your message or sound effect

3 Save the file to your computer. (It will have an audio extension, such as .au or .wav)

Accessing sound files

The Web is awash with sites with downloadable sound files. Some to try are:

Sound files can also be obtained from CD-ROMs and, in some cases, system Clip Art collections on computers.

- www.webplaces.com/html/sounds.htm

- www.wavcentral.com/

- www.dailywav.com/

Inserting sound files

Sound files can be inserted into a PageMill page in the same way as any other object. They can either be inserted directly into the page or they can be linked to a page, in which case they will only play when a textual or graphical hyperlink is activated.

To insert a sound file:

 Sound files can consist of music, someone talking or a whole variety of special effects, such as someone walking on gravel.

1 Select Insert>Object>Sound

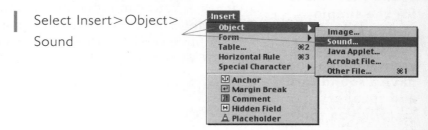

 PageMill supports the following sound file formats:

– .au
– .aiff
– .midi
– .ra, and;
– .wav.

With the exception of – .au files, they all require plug-ins to play.

2 Select a sound file to import

3 Select Insert

4 To include a sound file from an external Web site, add the URL here and select Place WWW Object (Link To in Windows)

 Sound files have to be previewed in a browser rather than in Preview mode.

When viewed in a browser, an icon for playing the sound file appears

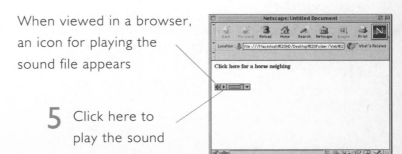

5 Click here to play the sound

Animations

Animations can be included on a Web page by taking a series of images and stringing them together in one sequence. This creates a similar effect to drawing several images in the corner of a writing pad and then flicking through it to create an animated effect. Animations for Web pages are created using GIF image files.

Creating animations

It is perfectly feasible to create your own animations and there are numerous programs and Web sites to help with this. Some to try are:

When you are creating your own animations, use images that only differ slightly from each other in appearance. This should produce a smoother and more appealing animation.

- www.animation.com/

- www.animfactory.com/

- www.gifworks.com/

- www.freegraphics.com/

- www.download.com/ (access the site and then enter 'animation' in the search box to select downloadable animation programs)

Using existing animations

Sites including downloadable animations are among some of the most popular on the Web. If you enter 'animations' or 'GIF animations' into a search engine you will be confronted with thousands of sites. It is just a question of searching through them until you find the animation, or animations, that you want.

The PageMill CD-ROM which the program comes on, has numerous animations for inclusion on Web pages. Look on the CD-ROM under Web Pages and Content> Other Content>GIF Animations.

Inserting an animation

Although a Web animation is a sequence of separate GIF files, the final image is just a single GIF file. As such, it can be inserted into a page in the same way as any other GIF image: Insert>Object>Image and then select the relevant file. These can be from a CD-ROM, from the Web or from the PageMill CD-ROM, which has a number of animations on it.

Video files

The one great drawback about including video clips on Web sites is size. They take up a lot of space and can take a long time to download. If you are going to use video clips:

- Keep them as short as possible

- Include a note about how long (approximately) they take to download. If it is several minutes then the users may decide they do not want to wait. If you alert them to this fact early enough then they will not feel as though they have wasted their time or been misled

- Be prepared for the fact that not everyone will be able to access them

Obtaining video files

It is possible to create your own video files but, since digital video cameras cost thousands rather than hundreds of pounds, doing so is an expensive business, and one that should really only be undertaken by the dedicated amateur, or even professional Web designer.

A more realistic alternative is to look on the Web. Try some of the following sites or enter 'video files' or the format extension (i.e. – .avi or – .mpeg) into a search engine:

- www.universesoft.com/vidcap.html

- http://softseek.com/Utilities/Video_File_Editors_ and_Utilities/

- www.webfair.net/real.html

A lot of video sites contain a large number of clips from popular television shows or films, which may be of limited use for your own Web site, unless you are a fan of a particular show and you want to include a relevant video clip on your site.

PageMill supports the following video file formats:
– .mov
– .aui
– .mpeg
– .dcr
   They all require the relevant plug-ins for them to operate.

If you are searching for video sites, you may come across a number of sex sites in your list of possible hits. These can be filtered out using a program such as Net Nanny.

Java

What is Java?

One of the favourite Internet buzz words of the 1990s has been Java. This is a full-blown computer language that was developed by Sun Microsystems in the 1980s. Its great advantage over other programs is that it is platform independent which means that it can run on almost any computing system. This removes the problem of Mac, PC or UNIX compatibility and it has led to Java being embraced wholeheartedly by the Web design community.

Java can be used for numerous multimedia effects, from running complicated animations to sending and receiving questionnaires. For information about the latest Java developments, take a look at the Web sites at:

- www.java.sun.com/

- www.gamelin.com/

Variations on Java

Web designers were quick to appreciate the value of a cross-platform programming language like Java. However, there was a perceived need to provide simplified versions. Hence the creation of Java applets and JavaScript.

Java applets are mini Java programs that can be inserted into HTML Web pages to create effects such as scrolling text, flashing buttons and animations. The usual compatibility issues apply to Java applets but it is a device that is becoming increasingly common on Web pages.

JavaScript is not the same as Java, but it is a closely related cousin. It was created by Netscape and in the programming community is considered to be less complicated than Java. Nonetheless, 'less complicated' can be a relative term as far as the uninitiated are concerned. JavaScript can be inserted into an HTML file in the same way as any other item. However, this requires some HTML knowledge so that you can at least place the script in the correct place in the file. As with Java applets, JavaScripts are readily available on the Web.

 Unless you are familiar with computer programming, the code for Java and JavaScript will look like complete double Dutch. However, this is no deterrent to inserting these items into your PageMill pages.

 Viruses can be inserted into Java applets so always run them through a recent version of a virus checker before you activate them.

Finding Java applets

 If you want an applet for a specific effect but you cannot find one to serve your purposes, then send an email to one of the applet resource sites. There is nothing computer programmers like more than a challenge.

Java applets are created in individual files that have a '.class' extension. The PageMill CD-ROM contains a number of applets and the Web is also an excellent place from which to obtain them. Some sites to try are:

- www.ccobb.org/javalinks.asp

- http://javaboutique.internet.com

- www.intel.com/cpc/webapplets/ (you have to register to download applets here, but it is free)

Once you have found a Java applet that you want to use on your site you can preview it and then download it to your computer:

Follow the on-screen instructions for downloading – see the DON'T FORGET tip

 Some sites have additional instructi- ons for what to do with the applet once it has been downloaded. Sometimes, too, there are notes on any additional items that are needed to help run the applets. Some applets are downloaded automatically when a link to them is activated.

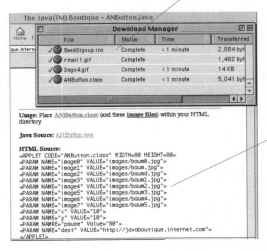

The code for the applet usually appears on the page

Some applets are downloaded as compressed files, which need to be uncompressed with a program such as WINZIP or PKUNZIP before they can be run.

Inserting applets

Applets can be placed within placeholders so that PageMill does not try to edit the code.

Applets can be inserted into a Web page and then edited to meet your exact requirements. To insert an applet:

1 In Edit mode, insert the cursor where you want the applet to appear

2 Select Insert>Object> Java Applet, then select an applet from your files

After step 3, the Java Applet section of the Object panel appears in the Inspector. Use this to change the dimensions of the applets and alter properties in the Name and Value boxes. Check the applet documentation for details about this.

3 Select the applet icon by clicking on it once, then see the HOT TIP

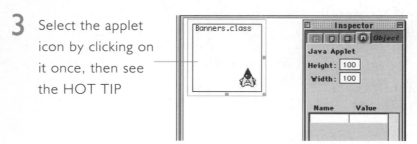

Altering how the applet is displayed in PageMill

1 Select Edit>Preferences> Java (Active Content in Windows)

2 Check on the first three boxes so that the applet can run in Edit and Preview modes

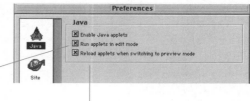

There are a number of applets available on the PageMill CD-ROM. Select Insert>Object>Java Applet and look under Web Pages and Content>Other Content>Java.

A fourth box (Windows only) tells the applet to look for more code in order to run it. Leave this checked off unless the applet documentation says otherwise

ActiveX

Inserting applets

If you are not familiar with ActiveX, it is best to steer clear of it. It is one of the more complicated areas of Web design and sites can function perfectly well without it. In addition, some browsers will not be able to run ActiveX items.

After step 3 in method 1, PageMill looks at the file and searches to see if there is an equivalent ActiveX control it can use to run it. If so, it will incorporate the file into that control.

For further details about ActiveX and downloadable controls, have a look at the Web site at: www.download. com/PC/Activex/.

ActiveX is a language that has been developed by Microsoft and in some ways it is their answer to Java. In Web pages it embeds programs that can carry out a variety of tasks, such as running multimedia objects or inserting calendars that update themselves every day. ActiveX programs are sometimes called controls. ActiveX controls can be inserted in two ways (Windows only):

Method 1

1 Select Insert > Object > ActiveX > Select File

2 Select an object file such as a video file

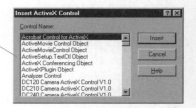

3 Click Insert

Method 2

1 Select Insert > Object > ActiveX > Select Control

2 This brings up a menu of preinstalled ActiveX controls, or files containing controls. This is not a foolproof method of inserting ActiveX controls because they may not all be functioning properly. If possible, use the first method if you want to include these controls

Using JavaScript

Before you include any JavaScript on a published Web site, experiment with the various effects for a period of time. Some items seem dazzling at first but their appeal can wear off fairly quickly.

JavaScript can produce similar effects to Java applets. Although it requires some knowledge of HTML it can be easier to use since it is included as part of the HTML page, rather than a separate file that is inserted and has to be run independently.

As with applets, there are dozens of useful Web sites for finding examples of JavaScript. Some to try are:

- http://javascript.internet.com

- www.webpedia.com/scripts/index.html/

- www.starlingtech.com/books/javascript/

- http://home.netscape.com/eng/mozilla/3.0/ handbook/javascript (this gives some background and general information about JavaScript)

If you are using JavaScript calendars, try to keep your page content up-to-date. Otherwise there will be a significant contrast between the calendar and what appears on the page.

JavaScript can create a variety of effects, from calendars that update the day and date automatically, to boxes that scroll the latest news items through them. Examples of these are:

Clocks

Calculator

Do not use scrolling text that moves too quickly. This can look jerky and be hard to read.

Scrolling text that moves across the screen

Welcome to The JavaScript Source! .....

Inserting JavaScript

When you find a piece of JavaScript you want to use you can do so with basic Copy and Paste techniques:

The HTML tag for JavaScript is: <SCRIPT>Place the script you want here</SCRIPT>.

1 Find the JavaScript from a Web resource

2 Select the script and copy it

3 Open your PageMill document and select View> Source Mode

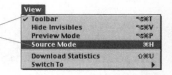

Once JavaScript has been inserted into a PageMill document it should be previewed in a browser rather than in Preview mode. This is because the JavaScript is run by instructions that are sent to a browser.

4 Insert the cursor where you want the script to appear and paste it into the page

The result:

The script is now visible in your active document when viewed in a browser

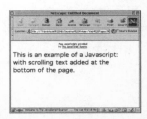

PDF files

Portable Document Format (PDF) is a standard that has been devised by Adobe to allow for the electronic transfer of documents that have to retain their original formatting. For instance, a newsletter that has been created in a desktop publishing program can be replicated exactly for electronic distribution, as can a complicated file of statistics.

For further details about PDF files, Acrobat and Acrobat Reader, take a look at the Adobe Web site at www.adobe.com/.

For Web designers, PDF can be an invaluable tool. If a document contains a lot of complicated formatting it does not have to be recreated in HTML, just converted into PDF. In addition, PDF allows for the following Web features to be included:

- Hyperlinks

- Online forms and questionnaires

- Password protection for added security

Creating PDF files

To create a PDF file you will require Adobe Acrobat. This can convert any document into PDF and then the result can be read on any computer, using a free Adobe program — Acrobat Reader. This also has the advantage of removing compatibility worries since PDF files can be read on any format of computer.

In Windows, Acrobat 4.0 can automatically convert a file from an Office application. In either Word, Excel or PowerPoint select File>Create Abobe PDF and the file will be converted.

Acrobat can create PDF files from complex documents (such as brochures and newsletters) that retain the original format exactly. They can then be inserted into a Web page using PageMill

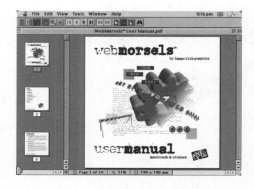

You can alert users to the fact that they will need Acrobat Reader to view PDF files. As an extra service you can also include a link to the Reader download on the Adobe Web site.

Inserting a PDF file

Since PageMill and Acrobat are from the same company, they integrate very well. Before you insert a PDF file it is necessary to instal Acrobat Reader. This can be downloaded free from the Adobe Web site. Once you have the Reader you can insert a PDF file:

1 Select Insert>Object> Acrobat File

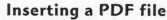

After step 3, a thumbnail of the image appears in the active window. The full document is available when viewed in a browser, if Acrobat Reader is installed.

2 Select a PDF file from a folder as you would any object or image

3 Select Insert

or:

1 Select Insert>Object>Acrobat File

A link to a PDF file can be either a textual one or a graphical one. If you want a particular item to act as the link, select it first before you insert the Acrobat file.

2 Enter the URL of the PDF file and then click Place WWW Object (Link To in Windows). This creates a link to the PDF file rather than embedding it into the active document. If the user has Acrobat Reader installed, the file will be opened when the link is activated

Plug-in overview

PageMill can run a variety of multimedia effects through the use of plug-ins: mini-programs that interpret different multimedia files. If you insert an item into a PageMill page that requires a plug-in to operate, the 'plug-in required' icon is displayed:

Plug-in required icon

If you have a very obscure file format then there may not even be a plug-in available for it . In this case, you will have to use something else.

If you try to insert a multimedia file, or any other file, that PageMill does not support then it will not be able to display the item unless a suitable plug-in is installed.

If this happens then you can either:

* Use another object or image

* Instal the relevant plug-in for the unsupported item

Most popular forms of multimedia have a variety of plug-ins available for them and so there should seldom be any problem in running them.

If the plug-in icon appears and the plug-in is already installed, the item should function properly when it is viewed in a browser.

Using hyperlinks

Hyperlinks are the lifeblood of any Web site, as they allow for a seamless progression from one page to another. This chapter shows how to create links using a variety of methods including straightforward links, anchors and image maps.

Covers

Chapter Seven

Understanding hyperlinks

Web sites are identified by their unique address, also known as their Uniform Resource Locator (URL). Every file on the Internet has a URL and these can be absolute or relative.

An absolute URL is one that includes the entire path name to the chosen file and this has to be used if you are linking to another Web site. A relative URL includes the path name from the source document.

The most common URLs are to Web pages (indicated by http:// at the beginning of an address, which stands for HyperText Transfer Protocol) but they can be used for a variety of other functions, including email addresses, which use the mailto: protocol.

Hyperlinks (or just links) are the threads that connect the World Wide Web and make it into a global network rather than just a collection of isolated pages and sites. They enable users to move around the Web, or an intranet, at the click of a button. Hyperlinks can be created:

- to another page within the same site
- to another Web site
- to an email address
- to another point on the same page

Hyperlinks are created by HTML coding which tells the browser where to go to when the link is activated (i.e. clicked on by the user). PageMill inserts this coding automatically, so you only have to worry about selecting the correct destination for the links.

Both text and images can be transformed into hyperlinks: in a textual link the selected text appears underlined in the browser, while if an image is acting as a link the cursor changes into a pointing hand when it moves over it in Preview mode or when viewed in a browser.

Textual links appear underlined
to indicate they are hyperlinks

Pagemill

An easy to use, WYSIWYG Web authoring tool. Available from Adobe it is one of the market leaders in Web authoring software.

On this page: Adding Text   Adding Image

Adobe PageMill 3.0

Images can be identified as links
when the cursor is passed over them

Creating hyperlinks

It is good Web design policy to limit the number of hyperlinks on a single page. If users are confronted with numerous links, they may become confused by moving to all of the linked pages.

If you absolutely must have numerous links on a page then add a note to remind the users that they can use the BACK button on their browser to return to the previously viewed page.

PageMill provides a number of techniques for creating hyperlinks in documents.

Using the Make Link command

This creates a link by using a menu to select a destination for the linking page:

1 Select the item that you want to make into a link

2 Select Edit>Make Link or select the Link (Browse in Windows) button at the bottom right corner of the page

3 Select a file for the link destination

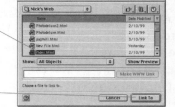

4 Select Link To

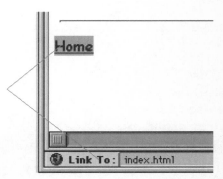

Since textual hyperlinks are underlined it is best to limit the use of underlining as a formatting device as it could lead to confusion. Use bold or italics for emphasis instead.

The selected item is now underlined, indicating that it is acting as a hyperlink. (When it is highlighted the linking destination is displayed in the Link To box)

Using the Link To bar

If you know the name or Web address of the file that you want to link to, this can be inserted by typing it in the Link To bar at the bottom of the page:

Be careful when typing an address in the Link To bar. If you make a mistake then the link will not work.

1 Select the item that you want to make into a link

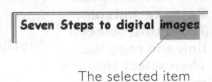

Seven Steps to digital images

The selected item

2 Insert the cursor in the Link To bar and type in the URL of the destination page

Link To: images.html

An inserted URL

With regard to step 2, note the following:

* If the destination page is in the same folder as the source page then you only need to include the file name

* However, if you want to link to a page outside your site structure you will have to include the file name and its location

* If you are linking to a file in another location on your computer then it is easier to use the Make Link command

The selected item is now displayed as a link

Seven Steps to digital images

Links can also be created by using standard Copy and Paste techniques. To do this, select a link and copy it. Then select the destination and paste in the link.

 With regard to step 2 in Method 1, the Page icon can also be dragged to a blank point on the page, in which case it creates a link with the title of the source page.

 If you insert a lot of links to the same page or pages then storing them on the Pasteboard is an excellent way to make sure they are readily available. However, you may need to edit the image or textual message once they have been inserted.

Dragging and dropping links

The usual dragging and dropping techniques can be used to create links between pages. This can be done by opening two pages side-by-side using the Window>Tile Horizontally command. Once you have done this there are three main ways to drag and drop links:

Method 1

1 Select the item that is going to act as the link

2 From the destination page, drag the Page icon onto the selected link

Method 2

1 Select a location for the link. From the destination page select an existing link and drag and drop it into the selected area

Method 3

1 Insert a linking item on the Pasteboard and then drag and drop it onto a page as required

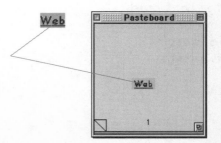

Linking to the Web

In addition to creating links within a single Web site, it is possible to link to any other page on the Web. This allows you to guide users towards other areas of interest without having to include that information on your own site. This could include:

To make them readily available, you can put all of your links to other Web sites on one page. Insert a 'Links' icon on your Home Page and then create a linked page that contains the external links.

- Sites offering background details relating to your site

- Sites selling something that complements your site

- Sites that you think are noteworthy purely from a design point-of-view

There are four ways to link to another page on the Web:

Dragging and dropping from a Web page onto the active PageMill page

1 Open the Web page that you want to link to

2 Tile the windows so that the two pages are side-by-side

If you are involved in e-commerce, do not provide links to a competitor's site – only link to sites that could provide you with a commercial advantage.

3 Select the item that will become the link

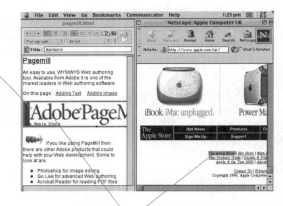

4 Drag a link from the Web page onto the selected item in PageMill (this now becomes a hyperlink to that Web page)

Dragging and dropping from Favorites in Internet Explorer or Bookmarks in Netscape Navigator

1 Open the Web page that you want to link to

2 Tile it next to the PageMill page

 Favorites and Book-marks are used to mark Web pages that are accessed frequently. The Web addresses are saved into the Favorites or Bookmarks drop-down list on the browser's toolbar. They can then be accessed quickly from this list whenever you want to view them.

This removes the need to enter the URL each time you want to access these sites.

3 Select the item that will become the link

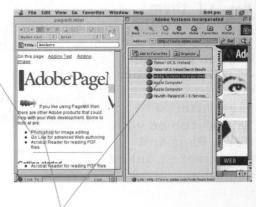

4 From the Favorites menu on the Explorer browser (Bookmarks in Netscape) select a file and drag and drop it to the selected item in PageMill

Using the Make Link command (Mac only)

1 Select the item that will act as the link

2 Select Edit>Make Link

3 Enter the Web address for the page you want and then select Make WWW Link

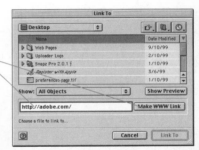

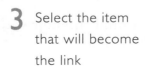

Using anchors

It is possible to speed up the URL entry process by using the TAß key.
To insert:
http://
type h and then press TAß.
After this, to type:
www.
type w and then press TAß.

Using the Insert command (Windows only)

1 Select Insert>Object>Other File

2 Check on the Remote URL box and enter an external Web address. Select Link To

Deleting links

When you are working with a lot of pages and links it is inevitable that you will want to delete and change some of them. To delete a link:

1 Select the relevant link

Pagemill

If you are deleting and editing a lot of links, keep checking your site structure to make sure you have not inadvertently created any broken links. See Chapter Eleven for more information on site structure.

2 Select Edit>Remove Link

Editing a link

1 Select the link

2 Select Edit>Edit Link

3 The Link To bar is activated – use this to change the link in the same way as adding a new link

Using anchors

Anchors (also known as bookmarks in other Web authoring programs) in PageMill are devices that enables links to be created to a specific part of a page rather than just the beginning of it.

Anchors on a single page

Anchors can be inserted on a page to enable the user to move around on that page (they are instructions to the browser to display a particular part of the page on screen). They are usually used on long pages that might have a table of contents at the top and the information below. Rather than the user having to scroll through large amounts of text, anchors can be used to navigate quickly around the page.

 When designing Web pages it is best to split long pages into separate files and then connect them with hyperlinks. In general, Web surfers do not like very long individual pages. But if you have to use long pages then insert anchors to navigate around them.

Anchors can be used to link a topic at the head of the page with the point where it appears in the document

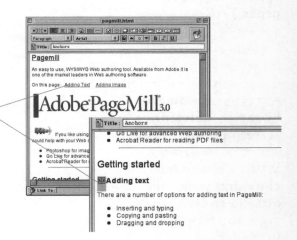

Anchors on linked pages

Links can also be made to anchors on different pages to the active one. This can be useful if you want to link to a specific part of another page rather than opening it at the top. For instance, if you are linking to a page of product details, you may want to guide the user to the price, halfway down the page. By inserting an anchor the hyperlink will lead directly there.

Anchors are an excellent way to add precision to your Web design and they are a feature that is often overlooked.

Inserting anchors

To create an anchor on a page:

 When using anchors, the link goes to the anchor rather than the text or image that is next to it.

1 Insert the cursor at the point on the active document where you want the anchor to appear

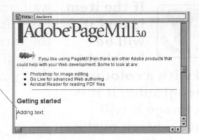

2 Select Insert>Anchor

The anchor icon appears on the page

 If you have a lot of anchors on a page include a 'Top of Page' link so that it is easy for the user to return to the top of the page without scrolling. Do this by inserting an anchor at the top of the page and then linking to it.

An anchor can also be inserted into an active document by carrying out step 1 below:

1 Drag the page icon to the desired location in the document window

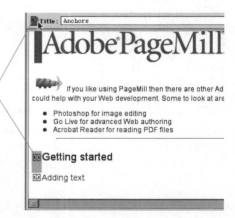

 To insert an anchor by dragging the page icon into the document, the page has to have already been saved and named.

...cont'd

If the item is text it will be highlighted with a coloured background; if it is an image it will have a black outline around it.

Anchors have their own individual names, such as "#anchor343423". It is possible to change this name so that it has a bit more meaning, which can be useful if you have a lot of anchors on your site or you are editing the source HTML.
To do this, click on the anchor and make sure the Inspector is showing. Click on the Object panel. The anchor name will appear and you can then over-type it with a more relevant one.

Linking to anchors on the same page

If you are working on a long single page then it is best to wait until you have completed the content before you start inserting anchors. This way you will be able to determine the format of the whole page and so position the anchors accordingly. Once the anchors have been inserted, links to them can then be created, once the page has been saved:

1. Select the item on the page that is going to act as the link

2. With the linking item still selected, scroll down the page until you reach the anchor you want to link to

Getting started

📖 Adding text

3. Drag the anchor up the page until you reach the previously selected item, then release it. (The text or image is now linked to the anchor)

Linking to anchors on another page

To link to anchors on another page within your Web site:

1   Open the two pages that are going to provide the link and the anchor and tile them next to each other

 Links to anchors have to be tested in either Preview mode or in a browser. Either way, the anchors are not visible, so you have to remember where the link is supposed to go to.

Anchors can also be hidden in Edit mode by selecting View>Hide Invisibles.

3   Select the item that is going to be made into a link

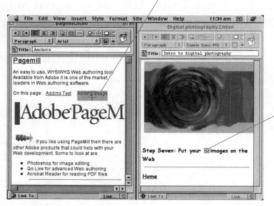

2   Insert the cursor where you want the anchor, then select Insert> Anchor

4   Drag the anchor and drop it onto the selected item, which now becomes a link

Creating a new link with an anchor

Anchors can also be used to create links on a different page, when no selection has been previously made.

1   Select an anchor

2   Hold down Alt and drag the anchor to where you want the link to be created on a new page

3   Edit the anchor's default name, as required

If you like using PageMill then there are other Adobe products that could help with your Web development. Some to look at are:#anchor491622

Creating email links

If you are including a link to someone's email address, make sure you tell them about it. Otherwise they may begin to wonder where all their additional emails are coming from. Most people would not give out someone's telephone number without asking them, so show the same courtesy with email.

Email is one of the most popular and widely used elements of the Internet and with good reason. It is a cheap, quick and easy way to communicate and it also allows for the transmission of images via attachments. It is increasingly common for people to give out their email address along with their telephone number, particularly in the business world.

Email on the Internet uses the *mailto* protocol to signify that a particular URL is an email one rather than a HTML page. PageMill follows this protocol and allows for email addresses to be inserted into pages. This is frequently to the Webmaster's own email but it can also be to various other individuals, especially if it is a corporate Web site.

To create an email link:

1 Select the linking item

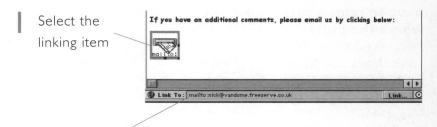

It is possible to pre-insert a subject heading for your email by adding: ?subject= XYZ immediately after the email address. However, this will appear for all the emails that are sent to this address via your link.

2 In the Link To box, type in the required email address, preceded by *mailto*

When the link is activated, the email program opens with the address already pre-inserted

Image maps and hotspots

Image maps can be used to insert numerous hyperlinks within a single image (either a graphic or a photograph). This is done by assigning 'hotspot' areas to parts of the image and then adding hyperlinks to each one. For instance, if you have a map of Australia, each state could have a hotspot drawn around it. When users click on an individual state they would be taken to a page all about that state. Although image maps are ideal for creating links to several parts of a geographical map, they are also very useful for groups of people or any graphic that has clearly recognisable elements.

 Some older browsers do not support client-side image maps and they can cause computers to crash.

When you are creating an image map it is important to choose the image carefully. If the individual elements are not clearly defined then the user may select a different link from the one which was intended.

There are two forms of image maps: client-side ones and server-side ones.

Working with hotspots

Hotspots are the areas on an image that are then converted into hyperlinks. These are created using a variety of drawing tools from either the Image Window or the toolbar in Edit mode. The hotspot tools are:

 The Polygon Hotspot tool is ideal for drawing irregular objects – create your hotspot as if you are joining up a dot-to-dot picture.

Rectangle Hotspot

Circle Hotspot

Polygon Hotspot

Shuffle Hotspot

Hotspot colour

Creating a client-side image map

Client-side image maps are easier to create than server-side ones and they usually provide a quicker downloading time since the image map and linked information are all stored on the Web page. However, the one drawback is that some older browsers do not support this type of image map. To create a client-side image map:

Hotspots are created in Edit mode and both the area of the hotspot and the name of the linked file are visible on the image. However, in Preview mode, or when the page is viewed in a browser, there is no visible sign of the hotspots. The only indication of them is that the cursor turns into a pointing hand when it passes over a hotspot.

1 Double-click the image to be used as the image map. (A lined border appears around the image and the hotspot tools appear on the toolbar)

2 Use the hotspot tools to draw hotspots on the image. (Each hotspot is given a sequential number)

With regard to step 3, use any of the linking methods described earlier in this chapter (except Insert> Object).
(The name of the linked file appears inside the hotspot.)

3 Select a hotspot and add a link to it

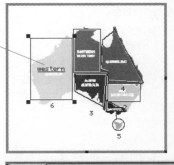

Creating a server-side image map

If you are confident about setting your server preferences and getting involved with CGIs then server-side image maps are a feasible option.

However, if you feel it is getting too complicated then it is best to stick to client-side image maps. Admittedly, there is the possibility of some people not being able to access them, but this is becoming less of an issue as more and more users upgrade their browsers.

If it is vital that people can access the links in an image map then consider presenting them in a different way.

This is the Inspector's Object panel:

Server-side image maps differ from client-side ones because the mapping and linking information is held in another file on the host server rather than on the page itself. This means that a browser has to go to the correct location on the server to find the relevant files. In some cases this will require a Common Gateway Interface (CGI) which is a script that fetches the information for the browser and brings it back to be displayed. In order for this to work properly various preferences have to be set in the Resources and Server menus. These will vary according to your Internet Service Provider (ISP) and you will need to contact them to find out exactly what their requirements are. What you will need to know is:

- The server platform
- The Web site map format
- The location of your site's root folder on the Web server (the Remote Root Directory)
- How to link the image to the image map file

Once these preferences have been set, the image map and hotspots can be created in the same way as with a client-side image map. The only difference is that the image map has to be created in the Image Window, not the active document window. After adding hotspots, close the Image Window, save the file and do the following:

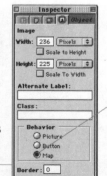

Click Map to have the image map denoted as a map rather than a plain image

Editing hotspots

Changing the hotspot colour

When you are working with hotspots in Edit mode the outline of a hotspot can clash with the background image, thus making it hard to identify the precise boundaries. In order to make hotspots clearer when you are inserting them, it is possible to change the colour of the outlines:

 Since hotspot outlines do not show up when viewed in a browser the only reason for changing the colour is to make the boundaries clearer when creating and editing hotspots.

1 Create a hotspot. (If it is on a dark background then the outline may be indistinct)

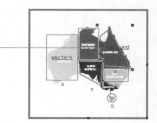

2 Select the Hotspot Colour menu and choose a different colour. (This now affects all of the hotspot outlines and also the text showing the link)

Displaying the hotspot label (Mac only)

It is possible to show or hide the hotspot label that appears within the hotspot boundaries:

Click on this button to show or hide the hotspot label

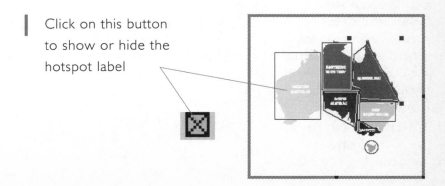

Try not to overlap hotspots if you can help it. There is very rarely a pressing need to do so and it can be confusing for the user.

 Once a hotspot has been moved it still retains its original numerical value.

 If you do not have a default link, make sure that it is obvious that the image on display contains hotspot links. Include a line of text above the image, saying something like:

'Click on a country to go to holiday information for that location.'

Shuffling hotspots

When hotspots are created the first one is given the numerical value 'I'. However, as more are added, each successive hotspot increases by one. So if there are four hotspots on an image, the first one that was created will be labelled 'I' and the last one to be added will be '4'. If all of the hotspots are clearly separated from each other then this does not matter. However, if hotspots overlap it becomes an issue. If a user clicks on an area with two overlapping hotspot they will link to the one with the lowest numerical value. If you want to change the order of overlapping hotspots use the Shuffle Hotspots icon:

1 Select a hotspot and then click on this icon

2 Select an option from the Shuffle Hotspot menu

> Bring To Front
> Send To Back
> Shuffle Forward
> Shuffle Back

Creating a default link

It is possible to add a default link for the areas of the image that are not covered by hotspots, so that if the user does not click on a hotspot then they are taken to the default link. A default link is added by clicking anywhere within the image, other than the hotspot, and typing the linking URL into the Link To box. You can then create a file with a message along the lines of: 'You have not selected a hotspot, please return and try again' and include a link back to the image map.

However, just because it is possible to create a default link it does not mean it is particularly desirable: it can become irritating to try and click on a particular link and then be taken to a different page entirely. If you think that the user may have problems with the image map, put a short explanation above it.

Formatting with tables

Tables are an invaluable device for formatting a variety of Web page elements. From standard financial data to complex text and image formatting, tables are one of the most versatile and effective ways to layout a page.

Covers

Chapter Eight

Using tables for formatting

As far as HTML is concerned, tables are made up of three main elements:

- **the overall table itself**
- **the rows that make up the table, and;**
- **the cells that make up the rows**

The HTML codings for these are:

<TABLE>...</TABLE>
<TR>...</TR>
<TD>...</TD>
respectively.

(TD stands for Table Data.)

Creating pages with wide margins using tables is a popular technique with Web designers as it creates areas of positive space and draws the eye to the page content.

Tables are a commonly used device on Web pages, although their presence is not always obvious. This is because tables can be created with or without borders so that they can be made to look invisible.

The immediate thought when tables are mentioned is that they are used for financial data, such as in a spreadsheet. However, while this is one use for tables, they offer a great deal more versatility.

Formatting financial data

HTML tables can present numerical information in an appealing and professional way:

%	Monday	Tuesday	Wednesday	Thursday	Friday	Saturday	Sunday
Team A	6.4	5	3,8	19	6.3	3.3	2.1
Team B	19	11	2.5	12	2	1.1	4
Team C	2.5	23	45	8	67	7.8	3
Team D	7.9	4.5	8	9.3	45	3.8	9
Team E	7.5	48	21	98	33	21	6

Presenting text

Margins can easily be placed around text by putting it into a table. This is a good technique to use since it guarantees that users will have white space around the text, regardless of their monitor size or browser settings. It can be made even more effective if the cell borders are removed:

%	Monday	Tuesday	Wednesday	Thursday	Friday	Saturday	Sunday
Team A	6.4	5	3,8	19	6.3	3.3	2.1
Team B	19	11	2.5	12	2	1.1	4
Team C	2.5	23	45	8	67	7.8	3
Team D	7.9	4.5	8	9.3	45	3.8	9
Team E	7.5	48	21	98	33	21	6

Combining text and graphics

It is possible to align text and graphics independently on a page. However, it is quicker, and more accurate, to design a table for the layout and then insert the text and graphics accordingly.

Tables are an excellent way to combine text and graphics to create the equivalent of a layout created in a desktop publishing program.

Table cells can be merged to create cells of different sizes and so provide a flexible grid for the layout

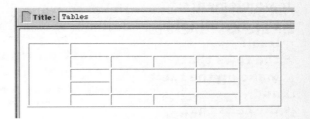

Creating complex designs

At first sight, some Web pages look horrendously complicated and many Web designers think they could never create anything so complex. However, on closer inspection a lot of these pages consist of nothing more than multiple tables. Once you know how to create and position them, the mystery of these designs is unravelled.

On some Web sites, the entire page content is contained within tables.

A lot of Web sites, like this one for the BBC, use multiple, or nested, tables to create pages with a varied and striking design

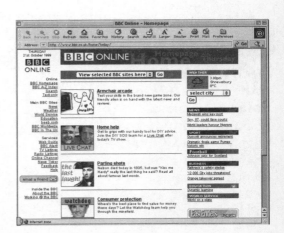

Creating tables

Tables can be inserted anywhere on the page and at any point in the authoring process. To insert a table:

Cell spacing and cell padding can be used to ensure that there is a reasonable amount of space between the items in the table and that they do not appear packed too tightly together.
   The higher the value for cell spacing and padding then the more subsequent space there is.

1 Insert the cursor where you want the table to appear

2 Select Insert>Table or select the insert Table icon from the toolbar

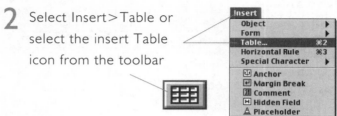

3 Implement the relevant settings in the Create Table dialog:

The number of rows and columns

Cell spacing: the amount of space between the table cells

Cell padding: the amount of space between the content of a cell and its border

Select OK when you have finished specifying settings in the Create Table dialog.

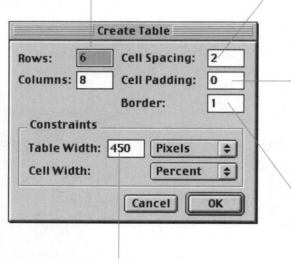

Border: the width of the table and cell borders. If it is set to 0 the borders are invisible

Table and cell width: this can be set as a percent or as the actual pixels. (As a percent it will appear in the same proportions on any browser)

If you want to have a table with invisible borders you will still be able to see an outline of them in Edit mode. Even if the border setting is at O they appear, but as dotted lines. This indicates where the borders are but they are not visible when viewed in Preview mode or in a browser.

The table is inserted according to the settings selected in the Create Table dialog

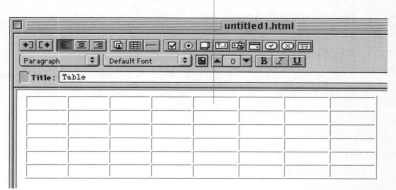

 The Object panel also has a caption function. If you check this on, a caption can be added at the top or bottom of the table. This is useful for items such as labelling financial data or adding days or months to a calendar.

(When a caption is added it appears outside the cell structure of the table.)

Editing tables

1 Click once on the table border

2 Select the Inspector's Object panel

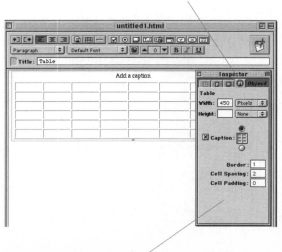

3 Make the relevant amendments

Selecting cells, rows and columns

For editing purposes, individual cells can be selected, as can entire rows and columns.

Selecting a single cell

1 Click anywhere within a cell – a thick line appears around the entire table

2 Click and drag to the border of the cell to select it – a black line appears around the cell

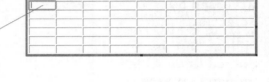

Selecting an entire row or column

1 Insert the cursor as above, then hold down the mouse and drag along the selected row or column

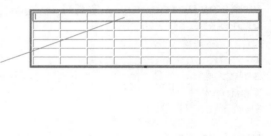

An entire table can be selected by inserting the cursor anywhere within it and then clicking once on the thick line that appears round the table. This then appears as a thin line, allowing the table to be resized if desired.

When a cell, row or column is selected the Table Cell panel is displayed in the Inspector. Use this to do the following:

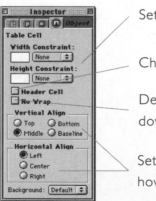

Set cell width or height

Change text to bold for a heading

Determine whether text can fill downwards or remain on one line

Set cell alignment. These options affect how text/graphics are aligned within cells

Adding rows and columns

Additional rows and columns can be inserted at any time, so that you do not have to plan the exact format of the table before you create it. To add a row or column:

 The functions on the Table toolbar can also be accessed by selecting Edit>Table.

I Select a cell as described on the previous page. This activates the Tables toolbar:

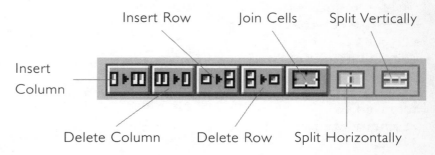

Insert Row   Join Cells   Split Vertically

Insert Column

Delete Column   Delete Row   Split Horizontally

 If you want to insert more than one row or column at a time, select the equivalent number of cells and then select Insert Row or Column. For instance, if you want to insert three rows, select three cells and then click Insert Row.

2 To insert a column, select a cell to the left of where you want the new one. Select the Insert Column button

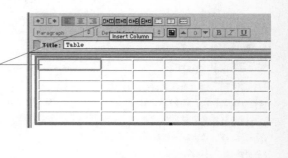

 Rows and columns can be deleted using the reverse of the procedure for inserting. With the cells selected, select the Delete Row (or Column) icon instead of Insert.

3 To insert a row, select a cell above where you want the new one. Select the Insert Row button

Resizing rows and columns

Rows and columns within tables can be resized by selecting a cell and then changing the value in the Height or Width boxes in the Inspector:

If you insert an object into a cell that is larger than the specified height or width, the size is automatically increased to accommodate the object.

I Select a cell, then change its height and width in the Inspector's Table Cell panel. (If the Inspector is already showing this appears once a cell is selected)

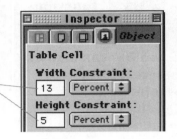

Changing one of the values alters the dimensions of the relevant row or column

Rows and columns can be resized when they contain content or before the content has been added. Usually, it is preferable to do the resizing once the content has been added, since you can see how it is going to affect the layout.

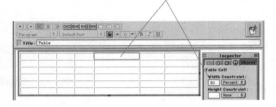

Rows and columns can also be resized by selecting a cell and then dragging one of its borders:

I Select a cell. Move the cursor over one of its borders until a double headed arrow appears

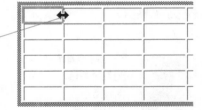

2 Drag the arrow to alter the dimensions of the row or column

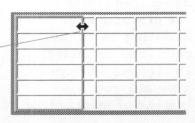

Some sizing issues

Some points to remember when resizing cells within a table:

- Each cell can be given its own height and width constraints within the Inspector. However, cells with percent constraints always take precedence over the ones with pixel constraints if there is any conflict. For instance, if two cells add up to a total of 90 percent of the table and a third cell has a pixel count that would be 15 percent, then it is adjusted so that it only takes up 10 percent and the pixel constraint is overridden

Try to view tables in at least two different browsers to see if there are any differences in formatting. Also, if possible, view them on different computers, because monitor size can have an influence on how they appear.

In this table the first two cells are set at 40 percent. Therefore the third cell will be set at 20 percent, regardless of any pixel setting entered

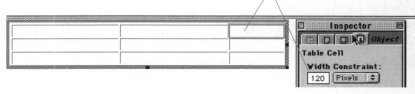

- Cell sizes may be interpreted differently when viewed in different browsers

- If the No Wrap option is selected then a cell will keep expanding while text is being entered. If No Wrap is not selected then the cell width will remain the same and the text will fill downwards, expanding the cell in that direction

- Cells always expand to the size of their largest item, regardless of the constraint settings

Adding content

Adding text

Most tables contain text of some description and entering it is similar to entering text on a normal page:

To change the cell spacing and the cell padding while text is being added, click once on the thick line that is around the table. This should bring up the Table panel of the Inspector. Enter the new values in the Cell Spacing and Cell Padding text boxes.

I Insert the cursor into a cell by clicking once. A thick line should appear around the whole table and the cursor should be blinking

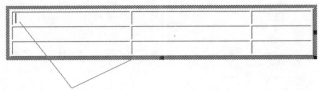

2 Type the text and make any adjustments to the spacing using the Cell Spacing and Cell Padding options on the Inspector

Text examples:

Text	can	be
entered	and	aligned horizontally or vertically
in	a	table

Text with cell spacing at 1 and cell padding at 0 (default setting)

Text	can	be
entered	and	aligned horizontally or vertically
in	a	table

Text with cell spacing at 6 and cell padding at 0

To edit existing text in a cell, insert the cursor at the relevant point by clicking once and then add or delete text as required.

Text	can	be
entered	and	aligned horizontally or vertically
in	a	table

Text with cell spacing at 6 and cell padding at 6

Text	can	be
entered	and	aligned horizontally or vertically
in	a	table

Text with cell spacing at 6 and cell padding at 6 and No Wrap selected

Formatting text

Text in a table can be formatted in the same way as any other text on the page:

1 Highlight the text to be formatted

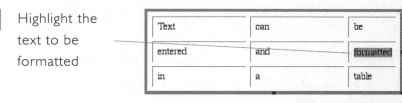

Text within a table cell can also be formatted using heading, paragraph and list formatting techniques.

2 Format the text using the Font, Size, Bold, Italics and Underline buttons

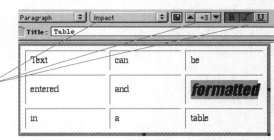

To select a cell with text in it, click the cursor anywhere in the cell away from the text. Then drag to the edge of the cell. The cell will then appear with a black line around it.
When you are dragging to the edge the text may become highlighted, but this disappears when you reach the cell border.

Aligning text

Text can be aligned either vertically or horizontally, using the options on the Table Cell panel of the Inspector, which appears once the cell with text in it is selected:

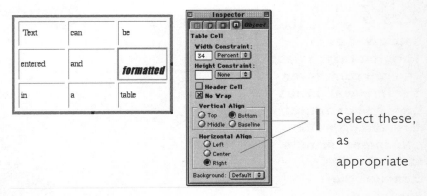

Select these, as appropriate

Adding images

Tables on Web pages certainly do not have to be used only for text and they provide an excellent way to position images on a page. To insert an image:

 Images in a table can be edited in the same way as an image anywhere else, by selecting them and then altering the options in the Object panel of the Inspector. This includes the height and width, alternate text and the border width.

| Insert the cursor where you want the image to be placed by clicking once in a cell. The cursor should be blinking

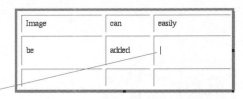

2 Select Insert>Object>Image

3 Select the image to be inserted

 Images can be aligned within a cell in the same way as aligning text. Select the cell containing the image and then use the horizontal and vertical alignment options in the Table Cell panel of the Inspector.

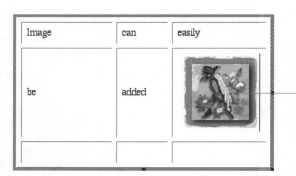

The image will appear and the size of the cell will expand, if necessary, to accommodate it

4 Resize the image by dragging one of the three sizing handles

Sizing handles

Joining and splitting cells

While some tables will need to be formatted perfectly symmetrically, there may be occasions where you want one item to span the width or height of two or more cells in the table. This could be to include a banner advertisement or to add some form of index down the side of a table:

When cells are joined, the content from the selected cells is combined in the newly created cell.

Joining individual cells can be useful for adding certain items to a table without changing the overall structure

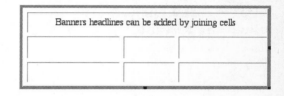

Joining cells

Select the cells you want to join (by clicking once in the first cell, then holding down the mouse button and dragging until all of the required cells are highlighted)

If two cells are joined and one of them has a coloured or image background, the newly created cell will have the site default background colour – grey unless it has been altered.

2 Select the Join Cells icon from the toolbar

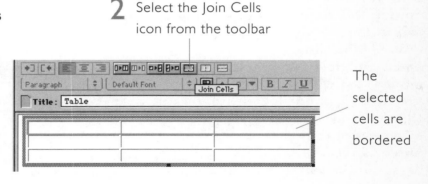

The selected cells are bordered

The selected cells are now combined into one, independently of the format for the rest of the table

Splitting cells (1)

Cells can be split using the reverse procedure to joining them. However, there are a couple of extra factors that have to be taken into consideration:

Only a cell that has been previously joined can be split.

1 Click once in a joined cell, but do not select it

Insert your	headline here	

2 Select Edit>Table> Split Vertically or Split Horizontally

The content to the left of where the cursor was inserted is placed in the left-hand (or top) cell and the rest is placed in the right-hand (or bottom) cell

If a cell becomes empty of content as a result of it being split, it loses its border. In Edit mode this is denoted by a broken black line and in Preview mode there will be no border around this cell.
   To restore the border, insert the cursor in the cell and press the Spacebar once. The border should reappear.

Insert your	headline here	

Splitting cells (2)

You can also do the following:

1 Select the cell to be split

Insert your headline here	

2 Select the Split commands as above or select the Split Vertically or Horizontally buttons on the toolbar

All of the content is placed in the lefthand (or top) cell of the newly split cells

Insert your headline here	

Adding background colours

 If you use a different colour for every cell in a table you will end up with a multi-coloured patchwork effect that could becoming annoying for anyone looking at it for any length of time.

 If Custom is selected in the Inspector's Color menu, this brings up the Color palette which offers a more extensive choice.

 Images cannot be used to create a background for table cells. If you try this you will insert the background for the whole page, not just the table. An image can be inserted into a cell, but text cannot then be placed over it.

Tables can have the same background for all of the cells or each one can have a different colour. To change the cell colour:

1. Select the cell or cells whose colour you want to change

Insert your headline and background colour

2. From the Inspector Table Cell panel select the Background arrow and choose a colour

The result:

The cells now have the new colour as a background. Text can be inserted over it and it is an effective way to highlight an item such as a heading or a total in a table of figures

Insert your headline and background colour

Creating nested tables

Nested tables are tables within tables and they can produce a professional effect, particularly if the borders are invisible:

It would be technically possible to create almost endless nested tables within the same original cell. However, there are good design reasons for avoiding this as the table could lose all form and structure. Three tables nested within the one cell should be seen as the maximum.

Nested tables

If you are using nested tables then it is a good idea to do a rough sketch of your page design before you start creating the tables. This way you will have a clear idea as to what you want and you should be able to keep track of things even if you are dealing with multiple nested tables. To create a nested table:

When you insert a nested table, if its width constraint is measured in percent, the table will shrink to accommodate the cell size into which it is being placed. However, if the width constraint is in pixels, the host cell will expand, if necessary, to accommodate the nested table.

1 Create a table and then insert the cursor in the cell where you want the nested table

2 Follow steps 1-3 on page 120 to insert another table, selecting the number of rows/ columns

3 Repeat steps 1-2 above for all of the nested tables you want to create

Designing with frames

Frames are one of the hardest elements of Web design to master. This chapter explains the concept of frames and demonstrates how to create them and add content to them. It also shows how links function within frames.

Covers

Chapter Nine

The concept of frames

Frames are a unique HTML device that allows a Web page to be split into two or more sections. Each frame on a page is independent of the others, so when you navigate around one frame, the content in the others does not move. This is ideal for items that need to be visible at all times, such as navigation bars or banner advertisements. Frames are used widely on Web pages and are a technique that is very popular with professional Web designers.

Having more than three or four frames on a page can complicate the design process and also make it confusing for the user. Two or three frames per page are usually the optimum number.

This example from the Computer Step Web site demonstrates the use of both horizontal and vertical frames

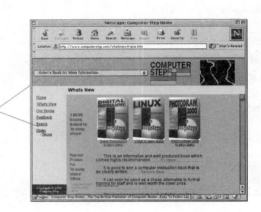

Frames can be used on a single page on a site, or can be a recurring theme throughout it.

Frames can appear either horizontally or vertically on screen and with or without borders. Numerous frames can be included on screen, but the more there are then the less space there is to display them. The advantages to using frames are:

- They are versatile and effective

- They create a professional effect

- They are a good way to combine different elements on a page

The disadvantages are:

- They are more complicated to use than a straightforward page

- They are not supported by some older browsers

Understanding framesets

A frames page uses separate files for each frame on the page. So if there are three frames on a page, there will be three individual files called, for example, *frame1.html*, *frame2.html* and *frame3.html*. However, if a browser was then directed to one of these files it would display only that file and the frames effect would be lost. So, in order to display the page with all three frames on it, another file needs to be created to contain all three of the frame files. This is known as the frameset i.e. a single file that tells a browser to display a particular set of frames in one window. So in the example above, the frameset could be named *frameset1.html* and when this was loaded into a browser it would display the files *frame1*, *frame2* and *frame3*.

 When you are viewing a frames page it is the name of the frameset that appears in the page title bar rather than any of the individual frames pages.

 To view the HTML source of a frameset page on the Web, select View>Source from the browser.
    However, to view the source for an individual page, Ctrl+click (right-click in Windows) with the mouse within that frame and select View Source (or Source) from the menu that appears. This will give the source code for that individual file rather than the whole frameset.

Frameset file name (this is the active document)

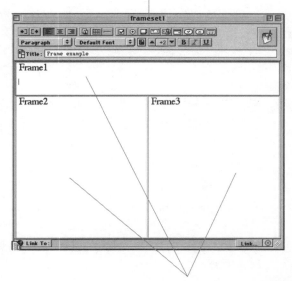

A frameset with three frames pages (each has its own file name, and the frameset is a separate file viewed by the browser)

Creating frames

Frames can be removed by positioning the cursor on the inside border and then dragging this to the opposite border of the same frame. A dialog box will appear asking if you want to remove the frame. Click OK and it will be removed.

The frame border can be moved once it has been placed initially.

It is best to create the design for frames and framesets before you add the content. Therefore it is a good idea to plan the layout of your framed site before you start creating it for real. This could be done with the traditional pen and paper, or you could practise creating frames in PageMill until you feel confident enough to create the actual framed pages. There are two methods for creating frames.

Creating frames by dragging

This method allows you to drag the borders of the frames into place and gives you a lot of accuracy as far as positioning is concerned. To create frames by dragging:

1 Open a new page

2 Position the cursor on any of the four page borders

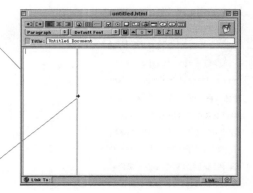

3 Hold down Option (Ctrl in Windows); a black arrow appears. Drag the arrow into the page to create the frame

Creating frames along the entire window width/length

1 Hold down ⌘ + Option (Shift+Ctrl in Windows) as you carry out step 3 above

Creating frames from menus

Frames can also be created with the Frames command from the menu bar:

| Open a new page and select Edit>Frame>Split Horizontally (or Split Vertically)

If you create a frame using the menu commands and you then want to create another frame along the entire width or length of the window you will have to do this using the dragging technique described on the previous page.

(If you try and do it with the menu command this will only split the active frame in which you are working.)

Two frames
created by using
Split Horizontally

Two frames
created by using
Split Vertically

Splitting existing frames

Do the following:

| Select a frame and then carry out step I above to split it

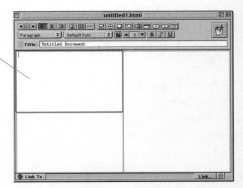

Saving frames and framesets

Once you have created your frames page it is desirable to save all of the components on it. This will give you a clearer idea of what you are doing since all of the elements will have meaningful file names rather than *Untitled Document 1, 2, 3* etc.

It is possible to save the frames and the frameset individually, or use a single command to save them all in one action. In this example we will work with a frameset that contains two individual frames.

Saving files individually

 The source HTML code for a frameset file will usually contain very little information. This is because all it is doing is identifying the files that have to be displayed on the page and as such it contains no content of its own.

1 Insert the cursor in the first frame that you want to save (a thin blue border appears around it, indicating that it is active)

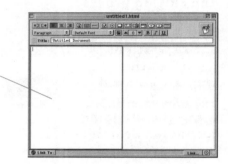

2 Select File>Save Frame and save it into a folder as you would with any other file

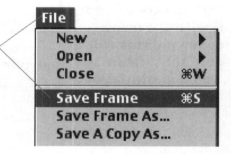

 If possible, try to give the frameset a name which identifies it as being different from the actual frames.

3 Repeat step 2 for all the frames on the page

4 Select File>Frameset>Save Frameset, then save the frameset into the same folder as the frames were saved into

Using the Save Everything command

A quick and easy alternative to saving all of the frames and the frameset individually is to use the Save Everything command. This automatically saves all of the elements within the frameset and prompts you to name all of them in turn. To use Save Everything:

The Save Everything command can be used at any time in the editing process for framesets. This is a good method of saving all of your work at once and you do not have to try and remember which frames you have saved.

1 From the active frameset select File>Frameset> Save Everything

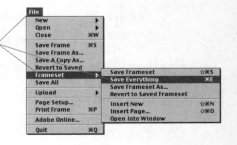

2 Name the active frame, then select Save

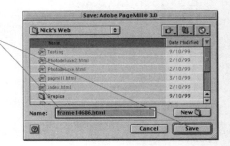

In Windows the frameset title bar displays the file name of the frameset and also the selected frame e.g.: frameset2:frame6 The frame name will change if you select a different frame on the page, but the frameset name will stay the same.

3 Repeat step 2 until all of the frames have been named and saved

4 The final item that appears in the dialog box is the frameset. Rename this and select Save

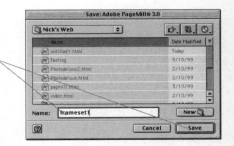

After step 4, the frames and the frameset are all saved.

Adding frame content

Frames can act as pages within their own right – it is only when they are viewed within a frameset that they take up a proportion of the screen.

Inserting content

Text, graphics and multimedia objects can be inserted into a frames page just as you insert them into a PageMill page. Select the frame in which you want to place the content and then do so with the Insert, Copy and Paste, or Drag and Drop techniques described in Chapters Three, Five and Six. The only difference will be that you will have less area to work on while the frame is displayed in the frameset.

Inserting other pages

The content on frames pages can also be created by inserting entire pages into the active frames document. This is a quick way to add content. Do the following:

The layout for a page that is inserted into a frames page will probably be different from normal, particularly if it is a small frame. By default, scroll bars are inserted if the whole page cannot be viewed in the frame.

1 Click once within the frame into which the file will be inserted

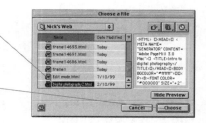

2 Select File>Frameset>Insert Page

3 Select the file you want to insert

4 Select Choose (Open in Windows)

To clear the content of a frame and insert a blank page, select File>Frameset> Insert New.

The file now appears in the active frame window

Opening a frame in a separate window

If a frame is relatively small then it may be difficult to add and edit content. If this is the case the frame can be viewed in a separate window, where it can be edited in the same way as any individual page. To create a separate window:

Blank frames can also be opened into a separate window and have content added to them. However, regular checks should be made to see how the layout appears when viewed in the frameset, to ensure it is acceptable.

1 Select the frame you want to open

2 Select File > Frameset > Open Into Window

The file now opens in a separate window. This is how the page would appear if it was opened outside the frameset:

Editing changes can be made to a frames page while it is being viewed in the frameset, but if it is a very narrow frame then a lot of scrolling may be required to get around the page.

3 Make any relevant editing changes

4 When you have finished making changes, select File > Save and then File > Close – the frameset will reappear and the amended file will appear in its frameset window

Formatting frames

There are a number of formatting options that can be applied to frames to alter their appearance and behaviour. These are applied from the Inspector's Frame panel, which is activated automatically when a frame is selected.

If the Inspector is not showing, select **Window>Show Inspector. (Click View>Show Inspector in Windows).**

Renaming a frame

By default, all frames are given a name such as 'frame23561'. This is not the same as the file name but it can be useful to change this to something more meaningful so that you can easily see what frame you are working in.

Select the relevant frame, then follow step 1 below.

Resizing a frame

In addition to dragging, frames can also be resized using the Inspector. Select a frame and then change a value in the Width (or Height) box. The values can either be:

- Percent, which is a percentage of the whole screen

- Pixels, which is an exact measurement determined by the number of pixels

- Relative, which sets the size as a proportion of the other frames. (If one frame had a relative value of '1' and the adjacent frame had a relative value of '2' the second frame would be twice the size of the first one)

Select the relevant frame, then carry out step 2 below:

The frame name is used by PageMill when other files are linked to a particular frame. Therefore it is advisable to rename frames before you insert links to them. This way there will be no chance of broken links being created, which could happen if you create the links first and then rename the frame.

1 Highlight the current frame name and overtype it

2 Change the value in the Width (or Height) box

To create a frameset where all of the frames merge together, deselect the frame borders, turn off the scroll bars and set the same background colour or image for all of the frames. This can create a very professional effect.

 Adjusting frame margins can create space around the content of a frame and produce a more appealing design.

 If there are several frames with narrow margins the content of one frame may appear to merge with that of another.

Frame borders

By default, frames appear with a black border around them. To deactivate this, do the following:

1 Select the frame, then check off this in the Inspector

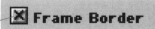
☒ Frame Border

If this is checked off for one frame then the borders should automatically be deselected from the other frames too. However, if you have vertical and horizontal frames on a page, select each frame and then check off the Frames Border box.

2 Select Save>Everything and then view the result in Preview mode or a browser

Margin settings

1 To alter the margin settings (the space between the page content and the frame borders), type revised entries in the Margin Width and/or Margin Height fields on the facing page

The default margin settings: Width 5 and Height 1

> **Seven Steps to digital images**
>
> Step One: Buy a computer
> Step Two: Buy a digital camera
> Step Three: Buy a

The same page with Width at 15 and Height at 20. There is much more white space around the text

> **Seven Steps to digital images**
>
> Step One: Buy a computer
> Step Two: Buy a digital camera

Only turn off the scroll bars if you are sure that the frame will be able to be viewed in its entirety. Remember that browsers and monitors display information in different ways and some users might not be able to view the whole of a particular frame.

 If viewers resize a frame in their browser this only affects their own individual view of the frameset. The changes are not made to the frameset itself and the next time it is opened it will have reverted to its original layout.

 Users can now resize the frame by dragging the border.

Scroll bars

If the contents of a frame cannot be viewed completely on screen then scroll bars are inserted automatically along the side or bottom of the frame. The default setting is Auto which means the scroll bars are only displayed if they are needed. They can also be set to appear all of the time, 'Yes', or not at all, 'No':

| In the Inspector, click Scrollbars then select an option in the menu

If scroll bars are selected and the borders of the frames are turned off then the scroll bar may appear to be 'floating' on the page and this can produce a slightly awkward effect:

If the scroll bar appears to be floating aimlessly on the page, consider rearranging the frames or re-inserting the frame borders

Anchors

If you want a frames page to open at a particular place when it is activated, insert an anchor at that point on the page and do the following:

| In the Inspector, name the anchor in the Anchor At box

Resizing a frame in a browser

Since frames impose a layout on users it can be useful to allow them to resize frames in their own browsers. Do the following:

| In the Inspector, activate the Viewer Resizable box

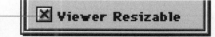

Adding a No Frames message

Since not all browsers are capable of displaying frames it is important to include a textual message to alert the user to this fact and to give them some alternate information. To include a No Frames message:

On your site, include a link to a page that contains the No Frames message.

Netscape Navigator 2.0 and later and Microsoft Internet Explorer 3.0 and later should all be capable of displaying frames pages. Since the majority of users will be using browsers with at least these specifications the issue of being able to see frames pages is not a vital one.
However, always include a No Frames message, since there will be some people who are still using older browsers.

1 Select Edit> Frame> No Frames Message

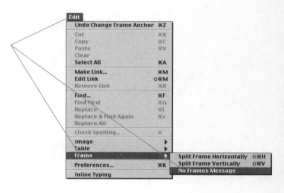

2 Enter the text that will be displayed when viewed in a non-frames-compatible browser

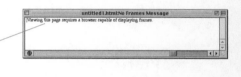

3 Select File>Close to return to the frameset

In a frames-compatible browser, the only evidence of the No Frames message will be in the source HTML code for the frameset page

```
HTML: Frame example
<HTML>
<HEAD>
  <META NAME="GENERATOR" CONTENT="Adobe PageMill 3.0 Mac">
  <TITLE>Frame example</TITLE>
</HEAD>
<FRAMESET FRAMEBORDER=1 ROWS="19%,81%">
<FRAME SRC="frame1" NAME="frame1" SCROLLING=NO>
<FRAMESET FRAMEBORDER=1 COLS="50%,50%">
<FRAME SRC="frame2" NAME="frame2">
<FRAME SRC="frame3" NAME="frame3">
</FRAMESET>
<NOFRAMES>
<BODY>
Viewing this page requires a browser capable of displaying frames.
</BODY>
</NOFRAMES>
</FRAMESET>
</HTML>
```

Targeting links

One of the hardest concepts to grasp about frames is how they react when hyperlinks are inserted and activated. This is known as targeting links and there are several options that can be selected when specifying how linked files will be opened.

Default

This opens the linked file in the same window as the link itself is in:

Look at sites on the Web to see the different ways in which links are opened in frames pages.

Clicking on this link displays the linked file in the same frame

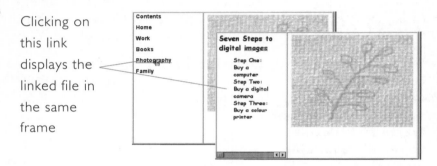

Practise with targeting frames until you feel completely confident with them. Be prepared for some strange results at times until you have mastered the technique.

New window

This opens the linked file in a new window:

With the target set to New Window, clicking on the link displays the linked file in a new window

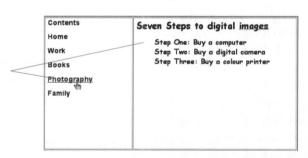

Parent Window

This applies when a frame is being viewed in a frameset other than its own. This can occur if it has been linked to another frameset. The Parent Window target means that the linked file is opened in the window of its original frameset, i.e. its parent.

Same frame

This opens the linked file in the same window as the link and is similar to the default setting.

Same Window

This opens the linked file in the same window as the link. As far as appearance is concerned, this looks the same as the New Window target. However, the same window option can be a better one because it is then possible to use the Back command in Preview mode or on a browser to get back to the original frameset. With the New Window command this is not possible.

Opening in another frame

It is also possible to target a linked file to open in any other window on the page:

Opening a frame in another frame is a common device when there is a series of links in one frame and they have to remain available at all times. In instances like this the links are opened into another frame and the frame with the links is still visible.

1 In Edit mode select a link by double-clicking on it

| Contents |
| Home |
| Work |
| Books |
| Photography |
| Family |

2 Control+click (right click in Windows) with the mouse on the selected link

When the link is activated it will open in the window that was targeted in the earlier step.

3 In the target window option box click on one of the thumbnail frame images

default
new window
parent window
same frame
same window

Setting a base target

Instead of setting targets for links on a page individually, a base target can be set which will apply to all links on that page. Individual links can then have their own targets adjusted if necessary, but the base target acts as a default. To set the base target:

When checking a targeted link on a browser, save the frame in PageMill before you view it in the browser. Then go to the browser and refresh the frame.

Repeat this each time you make a change in the source frame.

1 Select the frame or page for which you want to set the base target

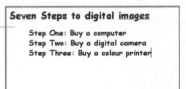

2 In the Inspector's Page panel, select Base target. Select one of the options to have this apply to the entire frame or page

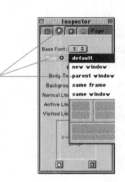

A link can also have a target selected for it by double clicking on the link, then Crtl+click (right-click in Windows). This brings up the Target menu and the relevant option can be chosen.

Setting a target for a link

To set a target for a specific link:

1 Select the link by double clicking on it

2 Select the target icon at the bottom right of the screen, then select one of the options from the Target menu

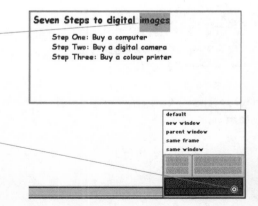

Interacting with forms

Forms enable Web designers to compile a variety of information from their users, from personal details to financial data. This chapter looks at how forms work on the Web and the various elements that go into creating them.

Covers

Chapter Ten

Using forms on the Web

Online forms should not just be thrown together on the Web: if they look cramped or unattractive then the user may just pass straight over them. Do the following:

- **Keep plenty of space between each item**
- **make sure the text is large enough to be read clearly, and;**
- **add some graphical objects such as images or horizontal lines for effect**

Also, do not include too many questions in a form: people can become bored with seemingly endless forms, whether they are hardcopy or online.

The concept of online forms is similar to that of hardcopy ones: information is sought through a form, the form is filled in and sent to its destination, then the information is analysed as required. With a Web form the process is a lot slicker than a hardcopy one where pieces of paper are sent backwards and forwards. The online form is designed in PageMill, the user completes it on screen and sends the completed data to the Web server, where the information can be extracted and acted upon.

There are a lot of potential uses for online forms:

- Questionnaires or market research
- Competitions
- Order forms for online goods
- Credit card details
- Passwords
- Entering search criteria

Forms also offer a different activity for Web users and they can make a useful alternative to looking at text or graphics, particularly if the form is well designed.

An example of an online form

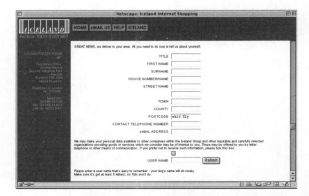

How forms work

The process of creating and using online forms consists of creation, transmission and interpretation.

Creating a form

An online form is created using a number of elements that allow the user to pick from a selection of choices or add their own data and comments. The elements of an online form are:

Use a variety of form elements when you are creating a form. This will make it more visually appealing and also more interesting for the user to complete.

- Checkboxes allow the user to select as many items as they like from a list

- Radio buttons allow the user to select a single item from a selection of choices

- Text areas allow the user to include their comments

- Text fields allow the user to include items such as their name

- Password fields are used to enter a password for the form

- Pop-up menus offer the user a choice from a menu

- Submit and Reset buttons either send the form to the server or clear the data from it so that it can be redone

- Hidden fields are used to store information for processing a form. They do not appear in the form itself

Sending and processing a form

It is possible to write a CGI script yourself, using a language such as Perl, but this requires a certain degree of programming skill. Alternatively, most ISPs have CGI scripts running on their servers which are capable of handling most form data. However, always check first before you publish a form.

Once a form has been sent to the server, using the Submit button, it is then processed by a script called a Common Gateway Interface (CGI). This can either send the form data to another location (such as your email address) or it can perform certain processing tasks with it. These can include placing the information into a database or creating a new page of data. Check with your Internet Service Provider (ISP) to see what CGI facilities they have.

Checkboxes

Form elements can be added using the Insert>Form command:

Plan the layout of your form before you start adding any form elements or text.

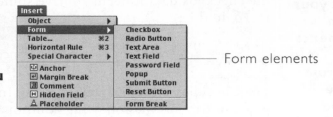

Form elements

or from the form buttons on the toolbar:

It is possible to insert a checkbox and then insert the text after it. If you are doing this in a row, make sure that each checkbox and the relevant piece of text are easily identifiable as being one element and that the checkboxes and text do not merge into each other.

Checkboxes are one of the most popular elements in online forms and they allow the user to make multiple selections from a list. To add checkboxes:

1 Insert the cursor where you want the checkbox to appear and type introductory text

2 Select the Insert checkbox button

3 Repeat until you have included all of the items in the list

The final list

Checkbox settings

So that the CGI script on the server can properly interpret the checkbox data it needs to have some values assigned to it. To do this:

Make sure that your form elements are easily identifiable from the rest of the content on the page.

| Select a checkbox by clicking on it once

The Checkbox options appears in the Inspector's Object panel. Carry out the following additional steps:

The entry in the Value box tells the CGI script the meaning if the checkbox is selected. For instance, if a checkbox is named Credit Card then the value could be Yes.
   Different CGIs have different value settings so check with your ISP.

2 Enter a name in the Name text box (this enables the CGI script to identify which checkbox is sending a particular piece of data)

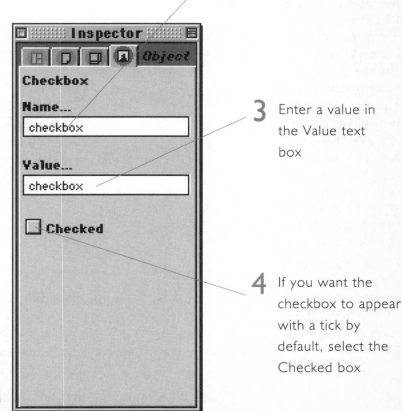

3 Enter a value in the Value text box

4 If you want the checkbox to appear with a tick by default, select the Checked box

If two or more check-boxes have the same name then the server may not be able to recognise exactly where a certain piece of data is coming from.

Radio buttons

Radio buttons are similar to checkboxes in that they offer a selection of options for the user to choose from. However, they differ in that only one can be selected rather than a whole range. For example, this could be used if you wanted to determine the method of payment for an e-commerce transaction. The options could be presented as radio buttons and the user could select the required method. Radio buttons are created in groups of two or more and when they are viewed in a browser only one can be selected at a time.

Radio buttons can also be added to a group by selecting the first button and holding down Option (Ctrl in Windows) and dragging the button to the new location. This creates a new button within the same group.

To insert radio buttons:

1 Type in some descriptive text for the radio button group

2 Insert the cursor where you want the radio button to appear

When you add radio buttons by copying and pasting or dragging, the most recently inserted button is the only one selected.

3 Insert a radio button using the Radio Button icon on the toolbar and add text as required

4 Select the radio button by clicking on it once

5 Copy and paste more radio buttons as required. (This ensures that all of the radio buttons are part of the same group. If you insert another one from the toolbar this will be part of a different group)

If you name a radio button before it is inserted this ensures that all of the copies that are made of it will have the same group name.

The entry in the Value box tells the CGI script the meaning of the selected radio button. Check with your ISP for the relevant values for radio buttons.

If you change the name of one radio button in a group then make sure you change the names of all of the others too. And tell your ISP of the change as this could effect the way the CGI interprets the form.

Radio button settings

As with checkboxes, radio buttons need to have various settings applied to them so that the CGI can process the data that they create. To create radio button settings:

1 Select a radio button by clicking on it once

The Radio Button options appears in the Inspector's Object panel. Carry out the following additional steps:

2 Enter a name in the Name text box (to ensure that each button is recognised as a group, allocate the same name)

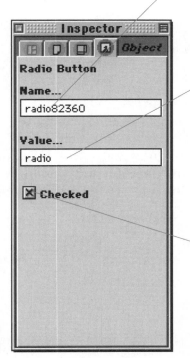

3 Enter a value in the Value text box

4 If you want the radio button to be selected, select the Checked box (when one button is selected, the others are deselected)

5 Repeats steps 1-4 as often as required

Text fields

Text fields can be used to insert a single line text entry, a password entry or a multi-line entry such as a comments box.

A single line entry

To insert a single line entry text field:

1. Insert the cursor where you want the text field to appear, then enter any introductory text and a description for the text field, such as 'Name'

2. Select the Insert Text Field button

A password entry

Passwords can be used to ensure that only a designated person can enter information into a form. However, this is not a form of encryption, which is a more secure method of protecting information and should be used when dealing with items such as credit card details.

To insert a password entry:

1. Insert the cursor and add any relevant text as above

2. Select the Insert Password Field button

A multi-line entry
To create a multi-line entry text area:

1 Insert the cursor and add any relevant text as in the two examples on the facing page

2 Select the Insert Text Area button

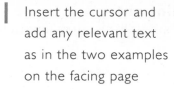

All text fields should be given a name in the Inspector before they are published, just as with checkboxes and radio buttons.
Select a text field by clicking on it once and this should bring up the Text Field option in the Object panel of the Inspector. Enter a name for the text field in the Name box.

Resizing a text field
When text fields are inserted they are created at a default size. This can be changed by dragging the text fields or changing the values in the Inspector. Carry out steps 1-3 as appropriate:

1 Click a text box then drag one of the resize handles

4. Please add any general comments below:

2 For text or password fields, amend the Inspector's Size and Max Length fields

3 For text or password fields, amend the Inspector's Rows and Columns fields

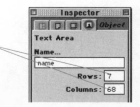

Pop-up menus

Pop-up menus give the user a list of choices, from which they can select one. This is particularly useful when there are a large number of options that would take up a lot of space on the page. With a pop-up menu, one option is visible and others appear once the menu arrow is selected. To insert a pop-up menu:

1 Insert the cursor where you want the pop-up menu

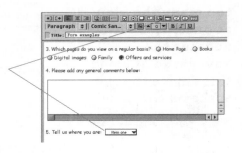

2 Select the Insert Pop-up button

To change a default item in a pop-up menu (i.e. the one that is showing before the menu is activated) hold and drag the down pointing arrow at the top right-hand corner of the menu. Drag it until you reach the item you want to act as the default and then release.

3 To add items to the pop-up menu, select the menu by double-clicking anywhere within its borders – a thick border appears around the menu

5. Tell us where you are:
item one
item two
item three

4 Select Edit>Select All

5 Type in the items for your list. (After each item, press Return)

5. Tell us where you are:
Europe
America
Australia

6 When you have finished, click anywhere outside the menu

List-selection fields can have as many options as you like but do not have too many showing at once. This rather negates the advantage of using this device to save space on the page.

 In a list-selection field, the default item is shown highlighted with a coloured background. The default can be changed by double-clicking on the menu box and then checking one of the boxes that appear next to the items. More than one box can be selected, in which case two or more items would be highlighted. In general, the first item in the list is the only one highlighted.

Adding a list-selection field

A list-selection field is similar to a pop-up menu, except it allows for more than one option to be selected from a scrollable list. To create a list-selection field:

1 Select a pop-up menu (created using the techniques on the facing page) by clicking its border

5. Tell us where you are: Europe ▼

2 In the Selection Field in the Inspector's Object panel, check on the Allow Multiple Selections box and enter a number for the Items Visible box

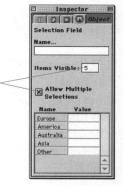

Pop-up menu settings

As with other form elements, pop-up menus have to have a name and value added to them so that the CGI on the server can recognise what they are. To do this:

1 With the pop-up menu selected, enter data in the Name and Value fields (but check with your ISP first to see what is needed for their CGI scripts)

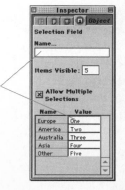

Submit and Reset buttons

Submit and Reset buttons usually appear at the end of a form. The Submit button sends the information from the form (not the entire form itself) to the CGI on the server for processing. The Reset button clears all of the data that has been entered into the form, allowing the user to start again. This is a useful option if you realise you have made a lot of mistakes and do not want to go back and correct them individually. It can also be used if you decide you do not want to fill in the form at all (for instance, if it involves a financial commitment of some kind).

 Submit and Reset buttons are usually positioned at the end of the form, immediately after the last response box.

To add Submit and Reset buttons:

1 Insert the cursor where you want the buttons to be entered

2 Select the Insert Submit Button followed by the Insert Reset Button. (The buttons are usually positioned next to each other.)

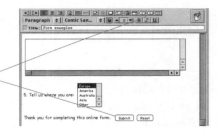

 An image can also be used as a Submit or Reset button. Select the image and then, in the Object panel of the Inspector, check on the Behavior> Button option. Now select the Form panel of the Inspector and insert a value for the Action the image button is going to perform (this will be used by the CGI).

Formatting a Submit or Reset button

Although they are functional, the words Submit and Reset are not the most dynamic way to end a form. However, it is possible to format the text for the buttons:

1 Double-click on the button – a thick border surrounds it

2 Highlight the text, then type in your message (the button expands accordingly)

Hidden Fields

Hidden fields are a form element that does not appear on the form; they are not viewed by the user. What they do is contain information about the form, or the way it is to be processed, that is passed on to the CGI when the form is sent to the server. One use for this is if users want the form data sent to their email address once it has been received by the server. In this case a hidden field would contain the relevant email address and the CGI would act accordingly when it comes across this information.

 Unlike the other form elements there is no graphical button for inserting a hidden field and it has to be selected from the menu bar.

To add a hidden field:

1 Insert the cursor where you want the hidden field to appear

2 Select Insert>Hidden Field from the menu bar

The hidden field is denoted by a purple H on the page (but it does not appear in Preview mode or in a browser)

 A hidden field can be placed anywhere within the form but it is logical to try to place it next to the element to which it refers.

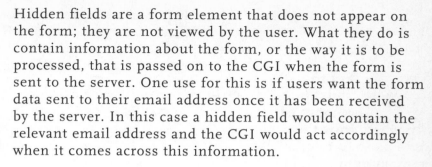

3 Select the hidden field by clicking on it

4 In the Hidden Field options in the Inspector's Object panel, enter values for the hidden field. (The Name and Value options are determined by the requirements of the CGI, so check these with your ISP)

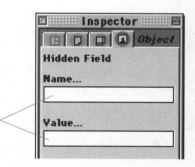

Multiple forms

It is possible to include more than one form on the same page and this can be a useful option if you have to gather more than one type of information. It is sometimes better to complete two short forms rather than one long one.

To include multiple forms on a page:

Try to limit the number of forms on one page to two, or a maximum of three. Otherwise the user may suffer from form overload and not complete them all.

1 Complete the first form, ending with the Submit and Reset buttons:

> Thank you for completing this online form. [Send to us] [Reset]

2 Select the Insert Form Break button

Make sure that each form is contained within its own section above or below the form break line.

After step 2, a thick white line (blue in Windows) with 'Form Break' across it appears below the first form. This is only visible in Edit and Preview

To combine two forms, click once on the form break line and then press the Delete button.

3 Create the next form below the form break line:

> Thank you for completing this online form. [Send to us] [Reset]

Form Break

Your TV and Film Preferences

l. How often do you go to the cinema? ☐ Weekly ☐ Monthly ☐ Never

Site management

Managing and maintaining the various elements of a Web site are an important part of ensuring the structure is as effective as possible. This chapter looks at the options for site management and shows you how to add, rename, delete and unlink elements on your Web site.

Covers

Chapter Eleven

Site maintenance options

Good Web design is about more than just putting your pages together and then sending them off into cyberspace to make their own way on the Web. Since the Internet is a constantly evolving medium you need to revise, edit and update your Web site so that it does not become out-of-date or inaccurate. PageMill offers a number of site management tools that help with the following tasks:

- Updating page content
- Renaming pages
- Adding and deleting hyperlinks
- Searching for items and checking the spelling for an entire site

To open an existing site, select File>Open> Open Site (Site>Load>Browse in Windows) and then select the site from your computer's folder structure.

PageMill groups together all the elements of a Web page and keeps them in one overall site. Creating a new site and opening an existing one is discussed in Chapter Two, pages 28–30. The site management tools have three different views of the information within a site and they all appear when a new or existing site is opened using the commands on the left.

Site Overview

This is similar to a file management system and it displays the site's folder hierarchy:

To return to Edit or Preview mode from the site structure, select File>Close (Site> Close in Windows).

Site Overview displays the folders, files and images that make up the site. It also shows items such as anchors, errors, external items and links to the World Wide Web

List view

This displays the contents of each folder in the site and provides various items of information about them:

File name   File type   Number of links from the file   Date last modified

The page title is not the same as the file name and if no title has been added to a page it will appear in List view as Untitled Document.

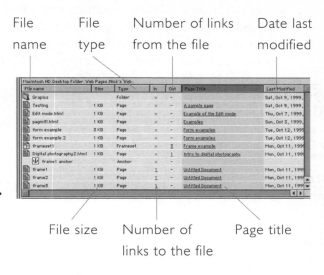

File size   Number of links to the file   Page title

List view and Links view can be used to change the linking structure in a Web site. This is dealt with in greater detail later in this chapter.

Links view

This displays the links to and from each file on the site. To see the links, select the file in List view and it will then appear in the Links view window underneath:

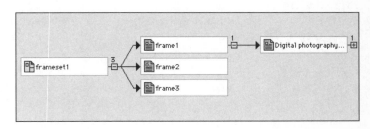

The number of links between files is shown e.g.:

Here, 1 link is denoted

Do one of the following, as appropriate:

1   Click ⊞ to view the linked files

2   Click ⊟ to minimise the selection

Navigating the site windows

If you make changes to a file in one view, such as changing its name, these will also be applied to the other views and the file will appear with its new name.

If you select a file in Site Overview, the graphical representation and the links to and from it are automatically displayed in Links view.

After step 1, the arrow is right-pointing – click this to expand the Site Overview.

You can also hide the Site Overview by selecting Window>Hide Site Details.

By default, the three components of the Site Details window are displayed together in the following format:

Links view

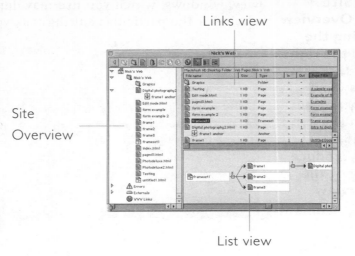

Site Overview

List view

However, there will be occasions when you will want to look in greater depth at one particular element.

Expanding or hiding the Site Overview

1 In Windows, click on the arrow to collapse the Site Overview

or:

2 Drag here to expand the Site Overview window

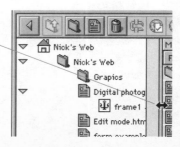

If you expand the Site Overview by dragging the border to the right, all of the List view and Links view icons may not be visible on the toolbar. If necessary, reduce the width of the Site Overview window.

You can specify the default for how the List and Links views appear when opened. **Select Edit> Preferences>Site** and then select the relevant icon as the new default.

If Links view only is selected then files will have to be selected in Site Overview so that their linking structure can be viewed.

Arranging List view and Links view

There are three ways to arrange the List view and Links view windows; which you use may depend on personal choice or the particular editing task you're performing:

List view above Links view (the default setting)

List view only

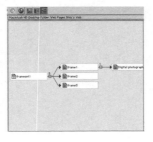

Links view only

To use a view, click one of these in the Site Details toolbar:

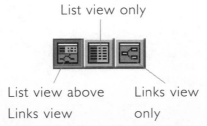

List view only

List view above Links view

Links view only

Adding files and folders

When you are reviewing your Web structure in the site windows, it is possible to add new files or folders at any time. This is useful if you want to create a new folder to put a group of similar items into, such as multimedia objects, or if you realise that you need to add some extra pages to your site.

Adding a new file

Web pages, images and multi-media objects can be added to a Web structure by dragging them from the Finder window (Explorer in Windows). Tile this and the PageMill site window next to each other and then drag and drop the items into your Web structure.

1 In Site Overview or List view, select the folder into which you want to place the new file

2 Select the New Blank Page (Create a New Page in Windows) button on the site toolbar

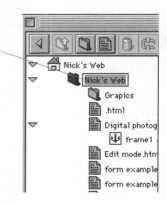

3 The new file is highlighted, with the name Untitled. Type a new file name and press Return

4 Double-click on the new file

The new file opens in a new window – add content in the usual way

Adding a new folder

New folders should always be created in the Site Overview or List view, rather than your computer's file management system. This way they will be fully incorporated into the site structure.

I In Site Overview or List view, select the location for the new folder

2 Select the New Folder button from the site toolbar

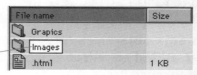

3 The new folder is created and highlighted with the name Untitled or New Folder – overtype this with your own name, such as 'Images'

Great care should be taken if you are deleting items: if you delete an element that has hyperlinks going into it then these links will be broken. Check in Links view to see the linking structure of a file before you delete it.

(If you delete a folder then all of the files in it and the links to them will be deleted from your computer.)

Deleting files and folders

If you decide that some files or folders are not needed on your Web site then they can be deleted from the structure:

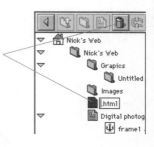

I Click on the item to be deleted and select the Delete button from the site toolbar (a cross in Windows)

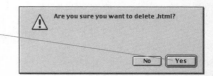

2 If you are sure you want to delete the selected item, click Yes

Editing files and folders

The Site Details window allows you to perform a variety of tasks that will be reflected throughout the entire site. These include:

- Moving files and folders

- Renaming files, folders or anchors

- Unlinking files

 A broken link is one where the browser cannot find a destination file once a link has been activated. This results in the browser returning an error message and it is a source of great annoyance to anyone who has ever surfed the Web.

While it is possible to perform some of these tasks in your computer's file management system (Finder in Mac and Explorer in Windows) it is strongly recommended that they are undertaken in the Site Details element of PageMill. This ensures that all of the relevant parts of the Web site are updated whenever a change to a file is made. For instance, if one file is linked to another and its name is changed, PageMill automatically updates the linking information. But if a file is renamed outside the PageMill structure then the linked page will have no way of knowing that the file name has changed and so the link will be broken.

Moving files and folders

1 Click on a file or folder, then drag it to its new destination

2 If the file or folder contains items that are linked to other pages, a special dialog appears – carry out step 3 below:

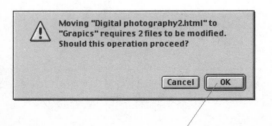

Moving "Digital photography2.html" to "Grapics" requires 2 files to be modified. Should this operation proceed?

Cancel   OK

3 Select OK to update all affected files automatically (to ensure the links are intact)

Renaming folders, files or anchors

When you review your site structure you may decide to rename folders, files or anchors within pages. This could be because the original titles were not clear enough or because as your site has expanded there are items with similar names that could cause confusion. To rename items within the site structure:

 Items can also be renamed by clicking on them once and then clicking on them again to allow the new name to be entered.
However, make sure there is a reasonable pause between the two mouse clicks. If you are too fast it will be interpreted as a double-click and the item will be opened.

1   In Site Overview, List view or Links view, Ctrl+click (right-click in Windows) with the mouse on the item to be renamed

2   In the menu which launches, select Rename

3   The file name will be highlighted – overtype it with the new name and press Return

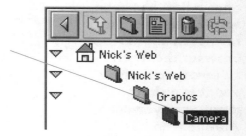

If the original file name was used in any links within the site the following dialog box will appear. Carry out step 4 below:

4   Click OK to continue – the relevant files will then be updated automatically

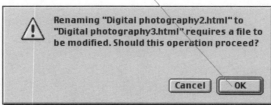

When links are created using this method there is no risk of them being broken. Also, it can be an easier way to create links because there is a clear visual representation of the links and the files involved.
   Once you have created links in this way, close the active window and save the changes. Click on the file in List view to display the new linking structure in Links view.

After step 5, the file item should now be a link – check in the Link To box at the bottom of the file to make sure the linking destination is correct:

This is an example of the Edit mode screen. This is where the text and images for the Web pages are inserted.

Creating links

In addition to the linking techniques discussed in Chapter Seven it is possible to create links when reviewing your structure in the site windows. This can be useful if you want to add a lot of links to different sites: the files can be opened while viewing the items you want to link to in adjacent windows.

To create links using the site windows:

1   In List view, double-click the file where you want to add links – it opens in a separate window

2   Arrange the open file and Site Overview so both are showing

4   With the linking item still selected, move to Site Overview and select the destination item for the link

3   In the open file, select the item that is going to become the link

5   Drag the destination item onto the selected item in the open file

Unlinking files

It is possible to remove all incoming links to a file. However, this does not affect the outgoing links from it.

Links view is the best choice, because this give the best before-and-after representation of how the site structure is affected.

To unlink a file:

1   In Site Overview, List view or Links view, Ctrl+click (right-click in Windows) on the file that is going to have the incoming links removed

2   Select Unlink

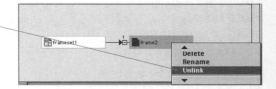

Unlinking an item does not remove it from the page. It merely removes the link.

3   To proceed with the unlinking, select OK

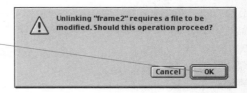

Before you remove incoming links to a file, go back and check that you really want to do this. If the link is going to the wrong destination then you could go to that page and edit the link.

The result:

Links view now displays the updated structure, showing that the incoming links have been removed

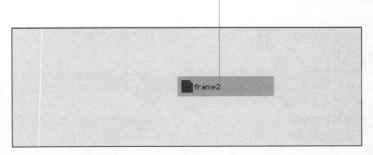

Searching a site

When you are reviewing a site, PageMill provides a facility to search it for specific items of text, URLs or objects and then replace them with new ones if required. This can be useful if you have used a company name throughout your site and then they go out of business or change their name, or if you discover that a URL you have used frequently has changed. To search a site:

 You can search for items in the source HTML code by checking on the Source mode box at the bottom of the Find dialog box.

 Spelling can also be checked for the entire site using a similar method to find and replace. Ctrl+click (right-click in Windows) on a file or folder and select Check Spelling. In the Spell Checker Search Path box select Page, Site Selection or Entire Site and continue the spell-check as normal.

1 In Site Overview or List view, Ctrl+click (right-click in Windows) on a file or folder

2 In the menu which appears, select Find

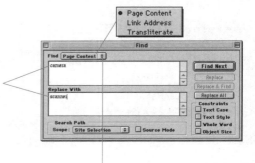

4 Enter the item to be searched for and, if applicable, the replacement for it

3 In the Find dialog box select whether you want to search a page, a selection or the entire site

When you opt to replace an item, it appears with a box around it on the selected page

Testing and uploading

This chapter shows the final checks that should be undertaken before your site is let loose in cyberspace. It also explains the settings that need to be specified before you upload your site onto a host server. Finally, the uploading process itself is illustrated.

Covers

Chapter Twelve

Testing a Web site

When a Web site is published, the files that make it up are placed on the server of the Internet Service Provider that is hosting the site. This is essentially just a large computer and when someone accesses the site, the files are copied from the server to the relevant location, called a cache, on their computer.

The final task before uploading a Web site for publication is to perform a variety of checks to make sure that all of the elements on the site are working properly. This includes:

• Testing local links. This is to make sure that all of the links on your site actually do link to something. The main reason for a broken link is that the name of the destination file has been changed. This includes links within framesets and image maps:

Test the links in your site by viewing them in Preview mode – click a link and make sure that the destination file opens

Once you have finished designing your site the immediate temptation is to publish it as quickly as possible. However, it is important to perform the checks in this chapter.
If you publish in haste you may find that you have let an error-strewn site loose on the Web.

• Testing external links. Since items on the World Wide Web change so quickly it is perfectly possible for links to external sites to become broken without you even realising it. Therefore it is vital to regularly check that these links are still valid

• Fixing errors. PageMill provides a number of options for correcting errors in your site when you locate them

• Collecting items that are located outside the site structure. This ensures that they are included on the final published site. These items are known as externals and PageMill has a specific function for collecting them

Verifying external links

If you have links to external pages on the World Wide Web then you are dependent on their authors: if they decide to change the name of a page then your link to it will be broken. It is therefore important to include verifying these external links as part of your Web site housekeeping.

To check links to external Web sites:

If you are checking external links, you have to have a connection to the Internet. When you verify your links, the Internet connection will be made automatically, as long as the modem is turned on.

1 Select File>Open>Open Site (Site>Load in Windows) and then double-click the site you want to check

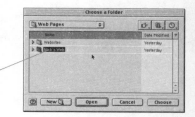

2 Click on the WWW Links folder

External email addresses cannot be verified in the same way as hyperlinks.

3 Select Site>Verify Remote URLs or the Verify Remote URL button (Verify button in Windows)

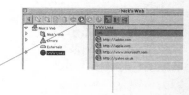

The remote files are displayed in List View

If a remote link has not been verified then the file appears with a red question mark on it in List view. After it has been verified the question mark disappears.

The external files are then checked on the Web and given an OK or Unknown Host/Not Found status

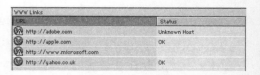

Locating errors

Broken links are the main cause of errors in a PageMill site. However, these can be identified through the Site Details window and then action taken to correct them. To locate errors within a Web site:

If a file is moved or renamed within the Site Details window then the relevant links will be updated automatically.

In Site Overview, double-click the Errors folder

The Error files are shown in Site Overview and List view

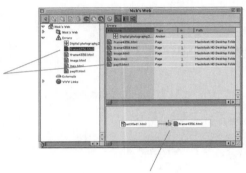

The nature of the error is shown in Links view

Error types are subject to the following classifications in List view:

- **Broken links are denoted by a red arrow**
- **Unlinked files are denoted by a red x, and;**
- **Unreferenced files are denoted by a red x and a blue dash (–)**

The PageMill error types
These are:

- Broken links – these are links that cannot find the destination file as it has been moved or renamed

- Unlinked files – these are files that do not have any incoming links to them on the site. This means that there would be no way of accessing the files, unless you have the full pathname

- Unreferenced files – these are files that have no links at all, either incoming or outgoing, so they would be impossible to open on a site

Fixing errors

You can correct errors in two ways:

Unlinking files

One way to correct a broken link is to remove it altogether:

 Files can also be removed in Edit mode. Select the link and then select Edit> Remove Link.

1 Click the file in List view

2 Select Site>Site Selection>Unlink or select the Unlink button on the site toolbar

 Once a replacement file has been chosen for a broken link, a dialog box appears alerting you to the fact that a file has been modified. To continue, select OK.

Changing the file reference

Another way to correct a link is to change the file to which it links:

1 Click the item in List view

| Errors | | | |
File name	Type	In	Path
Digital photography 2...	Anchor	1	
frame4356.html	Page	1	Macintosh HD:Desktop Fo
frame4358.html	Page	1	Macintosh HD:Desktop Fo
image.html	Page	1	Macintosh HD:Desktop Fo
inex.html	Page	1	Macintosh HD:Desktop Fo
pagIII.html	Page	1	Macintosh HD:Desktop Fo

2 Select Site>Site Selection>Correct Error or select the Correct Error button on the toolbar (not available in Windows)

The Correct Error button is similar to the Verify Remote URL one, except the former has a page with a yellow background and the latter has a white background.

3 Select a file from the Choose a File (Correct Error in Windows) dialog box, then click Choose

Gathering externals

If an external is collected that contains externals itself then a dialog box will appear asking if you want to gather these externals too. If you do, select Yes.

During the Web authoring process it is possible to insert files that are outside the site structure. This could include files or images that were already on your hard drive before you created your Web structure and which you subsequently inserted or linked to on your site. This will create a perfectly valid site, but because they are not within the site root structure these items, known as externals, will not be included on the server when the site is published. However, it is possible to gather together the site externals and place them within the site structure:

The triangle (or plus sign) means your site has external files.

1 If, in Site Overview, the Externals folder has a triangle (plus sign in Windows) next to it, select the folder

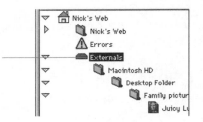

2 Select Site > Gather Externals

The Resources folder into which externals are placed is the same one into which converted images are placed. These are images that are converted into a format that is supported by PageMill.

The externals are now gathered and saved in the Resources folder specified in Edit > Preferences > Resources > Resource Folder

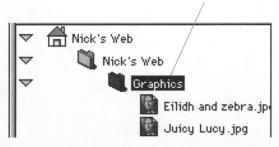

Site statistics

Make sure your site size is not larger than the amount of Web space that your ISP gives you on the server. This is usually a minimum of 5 Mb, which should be enough for most sites, unless they have a large number of images and multimedia objects.

PageMill provides two ways to view a variety of statistics about your newly created site:

Site content and resources

In Site Overview select Site>Show Statistics. The following dialog boxes appear:

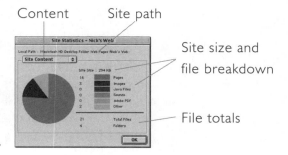

Content   Site path   Site size and file breakdown   File totals

To view the site statistics when in Site Overview, double click on a file to open it in Edit mode and then select View>Download Statistics.

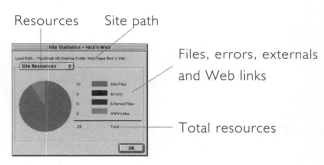

Resources   Site path   Files, errors, externals and Web links   Total resources

Download statistics

In Edit mode, insert the cursor on a page or select an object and select View>Download Statistics:

This offers a rough guide to how long a certain object, page or frameset will take to download in a browser with a specified modem speed.

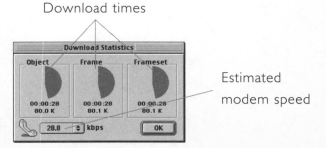

Download times   Estimated modem speed

Adding meta tags

No matter how good the design of a Web site, it will be of little value if no-one can access it. One way to let people know of your site's existence is to undertake a degree of marketing. This could be as simple as telling your friends, family and work colleagues of its existence and giving them the URL, or it could involve including the Web address in brochures, booklets, letterheads and business cards.

 Most ISPs have a limit on the number of keywords that can be contained within meta tags. Use a maximum of 50 keywords for each site.

Another avenue for helping surfers access your site is to include indexing information within your site, usually within the Home Page file. If you then register your site with a search engine this index will be added to their database. So if someone types a keyword into a search engine that matches one in your index then your site should be included in the list of matches that is returned. Indexing information of this nature is one example of an HTML meta tag. To add a meta tag:

 Use a variety of keywords within your meta tag – some that are very specific to the site and its contents and others that are more general and wide-ranging.

1 In Edit mode, select View> Source Mode

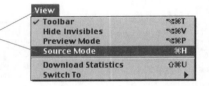

2 Insert the cursor at the end of the existing PageMill meta tag

The meta tag ends here

 Do not use keywords that are misleading or inaccurate. This will only cause confusion and irritation.

3 Insert the following item of code, including keywords that are relevant to your site

```
<META NAME="keywords" VALUE="Web authoring", "Vandome", "PageMill", "digital photography">
```

The identifying keywords are contained within quotation marks

Site settings

The process of uploading a site is known as File Transfer Protocol (FTP).

Most ISPs have online instructions for entering basic FTP information. Try looking under Technical Support or Online Help on the ISP's Home Page.

If you have any queries about your FTP settings, try contacting your ISP by email rather than the expensive telephone hotline.

The Site Settings dialog box can be accessed through either Site Overview or Edit mode.

Once you have created and checked your site it is time to publish it on the World Wide Web. This is known as uploading the site. Although the process of uploading is a relatively straightforward one there are a number of settings to specify before the site is uploaded to the host server. To make sure that these settings are compatible with the server it will be necessary to contact the Internet Service Provider (ISP) who will be hosting your site. Your ISP's Home Page may have information about uploading a Web site, or they may be able to send you written documentation. Either way, study this information carefully as it could have important consequences for your site.

Adjusting basic settings

The basic settings that you will have to specify for uploading are (you will have to get these from your ISP):

- Host name

- User name

- Password

- Remote folder (with some ISPs this is left blank)

These are added in the Add Site Settings dialog box which is accessed by selecting Site>Show Settings, then selecting a site and clicking on Edit:

1 Ensure General is active

2 Enter the name of the Web site and its location on your computer

3 Obtain this information from your ISP or Web administrator (these are the FTP settings)

4 Click here

The extra menus are accessed through Edit mode by selecting Site>Show Settings and then choosing a site and selecting Edit.

You should not change any of the advanced settings unless you have good reason to do so. The most likely change to make is the one for uploading files. After the site has been loaded for the first time, you may want to change the setting to Upload Modified Files (Newer Files in Windows) so that only files that have been amended are uploaded each time you load files onto the server.

After each step 1, carry out step 4 on page 183.

There are three additional menus that offer various advanced settings:

The Advanced menu

The Advanced menu determines which files are uploaded. The options are:

- Upload All Files (Always in Windows)

- Upload Modified Files (Newer Files in Windows)

- Synchronize (Synchronize Files in Windows) which updates newer files on the Web Server and on the local directory

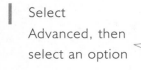
Select Advanced, then select an option

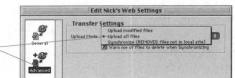

The ASCII menu

For some files with certain extensions you may want to transfer them using ASCII transfer:

Select ASCII, then type in the full file extension

The Ignore menu

Select Ignore, then enter the extension of file types you want to exclude

Uploading a site

Try and keep your filenames to eight characters and do not use spaces. Also keep the 'Treat Case-Sensitive URL Differences as Errors' checked on in the Resources panel of the Preferences menu. This should avoid any problems with case-sensitive servers.

PageMill has a built in FTP facility for uploading pages onto the server. This means that you do not need a separate FTP program to upload your site. If all of the site settings have already been specified it will make the uploading process quicker but they can be added during the uploading process.

To upload a site:

1 Select Site>Load and then load the site to be uploaded

2 In the site details window select Site>Upload

3 The site settings that were determined on page 183 should now appear – select OK

On the PC, the loading statistics also include:

- **the transfer rate, and;**
- **the approximate time left for downloading**

Mac

As the site loads, a status dialog window appears, showing loading statistics

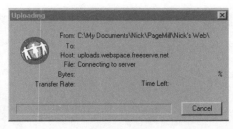

PC

Uploading single items

After a Web site has been published for the first time it is important to add new items and update the pages that have already been created. This keeps the site fresh and current and it should, hopefully, persuade people to keep revisiting it to see what has been added.

PageMill provides a facility to upload individual items, without the need to reload the whole site again. This can include files, objects and framesets.

Uploading a page or a frameset

When you upload a single item, PageMill automatically includes any associated files or objects.

1 Open the page or frameset in Edit mode

2 Select File>Upload>Page (or Frameset)

3 Proceed in the same way as for an entire site

Uploading a single object

1 In Edit mode, select the object to be uploaded

2 Select File>Upload>Object

3 Proceed in the same way as for an entire site

Uploading items in Site Overview

An alternative to uploading individual items in Edit mode is to use Site Overview:

Unlike uploading a specific item in Edit mode, the technique on the right only loads the selected item, not any elements that are linked to it.

1 With the site loaded, select the item, or items, that you want to upload

2 Select Site>Site Selection>Upload

3 Proceed in the same way as for an entire site

Index

U

V

W